Rust Networking

A Step-by-Step Guide to Building Safe, Concurrent, and Efficient Network Services

Jeffrey Muniz

All rights reserved. No part of this book may be reproduced, stored in a retrieval system, or transmitted, in any form or by any means, electronic, mechanical, photocopying, recording, or otherwise, without the prior written permission of the author, except in the case of brief quotations embodied in critical reviews and certain other noncommercial uses permitted by copyright law.

Copyright © 2024 Jeffrey Muniz

Table of contents

Preface.. 6
Chapter 1: Introduction.. 8
   1.1 Why Rust for Network Programming?............................ 8
   1.2 Network Fundamentals.. 12
   1.3 Setting Up Your Environment.. 25
       1.3.1 Installing Rust.. 26
       1.3.2 Choosing a Code Editor or IDE............................. 27
       1.3.3 Managing Dependencies with Cargo.................... 27
       1.3.4 Exploring the Rust Ecosystem.............................. 29
Chapter 2: Rust Essentials for Networking........................ 30
   2.1 Working with Data... 30
       2.1.1 Primitive Data Types... 30
       2.1.2 Strings and Byte Arrays.. 34
       2.1.3 Structs and Enums... 38
   2.2 Error Handling... 43
   2.3 Memory Management and Ownership.......................... 48
   2.4 Introduction to Concurrency with Threads.................... 52
Chapter 3: Sockets and Low-Level Networking................ 57
   3.1 The std::net Module.. 57
   3.2 TCP Sockets... 61
   3.3 UDP Sockets... 73
   3.4 Socket Options and Configuration................................ 76
Chapter 4: Asynchronous Programming with Tokio........ 81
   4.1 Introduction to Asynchronous Programming................ 81
   4.2 The Tokio Runtime.. 84
   4.3 Futures, Tasks, and Executors..................................... 87
   4.4 Asynchronous TCP and UDP Sockets.......................... 91
   4.5 Handling Multiple Connections Concurrently............... 95
Chapter 5: Serialization and Deserialization................... 100
   5.1 JSON with serde_json.. 100
   5.2 Other Serialization Formats... 112
   5.3 Custom Serialization.. 118
Chapter 6: Building a Robust Web Server....................... 123
   6.1 HTTP and Request/Response Cycle............................ 123

    6.2 Building a Basic HTTP Server with hyper................................. 126
    6.3 Routing and Handling Requests... 129
    6.4 Serving Static Files... 133
    6.5 Handling Data with Templates.. 137
Chapter 7: Advanced Concurrency Patterns...................................... 142
    7.1 Channels for Communication.. 142
    7.2 Shared State and Synchronization... 145
    7.3 Thread Pools and Work Stealing.. 149
    7.4 Asynchronous Streams...152
Chapter 8: Network Security... 156
    8.1 Transport Layer Security... 157
    8.2 Encryption and Decryption..161
    8.3 Authentication and Authorization... 165
Chapter 9: Building a Real-time Chat Application...........................170
    9.1 WebSockets..170
    9.2 Handling Multiple Users and Chat Rooms................................ 174
    9.3 Broadcasting Messages... 178
Chapter 10: Performance Optimization... 181
    10.1 Profiling and Benchmarking... 182
    10.2 Buffering Strategies.. 185
    10.3 Multiplexing and I/O Models... 188
    10.4 Zero-Copy Networking.. 191
Chapter 11: Testing and Debugging... 194
    11.1 Unit Testing.. 195
    11.2 Integration Testing..199
    11.3 Debugging Techniques.. 203
Chapter 12: Deployment and Monitoring... 206
    12.1 Deploying to a Server.. 207
    12.2 Monitoring and Logging.. 211
Conclusion..214

Preface

Ever felt that itch to build something *really* cool with Rust? Something that connects people, shares information, and maybe even changes how we interact online? Well, you've come to the right place. This book is your guide to the exciting domain of network programming with Rust – a language that's quickly becoming a favorite for building safe, reliable, and blazingly fast network applications.

Background and Motivation

Let's be honest, network programming can be a bit intimidating. Dealing with sockets, protocols, concurrency – it can feel like a jungle out there! But fear not, because Rust comes to the rescue with its superpowers: memory safety, fearless concurrency, and performance that'll make your applications fly. This book was born out of a desire to demystify network programming and empower Rustaceans like you to create amazing things.

Purpose and Scope

This book aims to be your one-stop shop for learning how to build a wide range of network applications with Rust. We'll start with the basics, laying a solid foundation in network fundamentals and essential Rust concepts. Then, we'll progressively explore more advanced topics, like asynchronous programming, security, and performance optimization. By the end, you'll have the knowledge and confidence to tackle real-world projects, whether it's building a high-performance web server, a real-time chat application, or even a networked game.

Target Audience

This book is perfect for you if:

- You're a Rust programmer who wants to expand your skills into network programming.
- You have some experience with network programming in other languages and are curious about how Rust can make things easier and safer.
- You're excited about building robust, efficient, and concurrent network applications.

Whether you're a student, a hobbyist, or a seasoned professional, you'll find valuable insights and practical guidance within these pages.

Organization and Structure

This book is organized in a way that allows you to learn progressively. We'll start with foundational concepts and gradually build upon them, introducing new tools and techniques as we go. Each chapter is packed with clear explanations, practical examples, and hands-on exercises to solidify your understanding. We'll also explore real-world applications, showing you how to put your newfound knowledge into practice.

So, are you ready to embark on this exciting adventure? Get ready to unlock the power of Rust and build some truly amazing network applications. Let's get started!

Chapter 1: Introduction

Alright, let's kick things off! In this chapter, we'll set the stage for our exciting journey into the world of network programming with Rust. We'll explore why Rust is such a fantastic choice for building network applications, refresh some core networking concepts, and get your development environment ready to roll.

1.1 Why Rust for Network Programming?

You're probably curious why we're focusing on Rust for network programming. After all, languages like C, C++, Java, and Python have been used for network tasks for decades. While these languages certainly have their merits, Rust brings a unique combination of features to the table that make it exceptionally well-suited for building robust, efficient, and secure network applications. Let's explore these advantages in detail.

Memory Safety

One of the most significant challenges in network programming, particularly when using languages like C and C++, is ensuring memory safety. Memory safety means preventing bugs that can corrupt memory, such as buffer overflows, dangling pointers, and use-after-free errors. These bugs can lead to crashes, unpredictable behavior, and even security vulnerabilities that attackers can exploit.

Rust tackles this challenge head-on with its innovative ownership and borrowing system. The compiler acts as a strict enforcer, ensuring that you access and modify memory in a safe and controlled manner. This eliminates entire classes of memory-related errors at compile time, saving you countless hours of debugging and making your network applications far more reliable.

What's remarkable is that Rust achieves this memory safety without relying on garbage collection. Garbage collection, while convenient, can introduce performance overhead and unpredictable pauses, which are often undesirable in network applications that demand low latency and consistent responsiveness. Rust's compile-time checks provide the best of both worlds: memory safety and performance.

Concurrency

Network applications often need to handle multiple connections, process data streams, and perform various tasks concurrently. Concurrency, while essential, can be notoriously difficult to get right. Traditional approaches using threads and locks can easily lead to data races, deadlocks, and other concurrency bugs that are incredibly challenging to track down and fix.

Rust empowers you to write concurrent code with confidence. Its ownership and borrowing system prevents data races at compile time, ensuring that multiple threads can access data safely without the risk of corruption. Moreover, Rust provides high-level concurrency primitives, such as channels and asynchronous programming features, that make it easier to express complex concurrent logic in a clear and manageable way.

For instance, let's say you're building a chat server that needs to handle hundreds or even thousands of concurrent users. With Rust, you can leverage its concurrency features to create a highly efficient and scalable server that can handle the load without breaking a sweat.

```
Rust

use std::sync::mpsc;

use std::thread;
```

```
fn main() {
    let (tx, rx) = mpsc::channel();
    thread::spawn(move || {
        let val = String::from("hello");
        tx.send(val).unwrap();[1]
    });
    let received = rx.recv().unwrap();
    println!("Got: {}", received);[2]
}
```

In this example, we use a channel (mpsc) to send a message between two threads. The send() method sends the message, and the recv() method receives it. Rust's type system and ownership rules ensure that this communication is safe and free from data races.

Performance

When it comes to network programming, performance is often critical. Network applications need to handle high volumes of data, respond quickly to requests, and minimize latency to provide a smooth user experience.

Rust excels in this area by compiling to native code, just like C and C++. This means your Rust network applications can achieve performance comparable to these lower-level languages, without sacrificing safety or expressiveness. Rust's zero-cost abstractions and efficient memory management contribute to its impressive performance characteristics.

Consider a scenario where you're building a high-performance web server. Rust's speed and efficiency allow you to handle a large number of concurrent requests without sacrificing responsiveness or consuming excessive resources. This translates to a better experience for your users and lower operating costs.

A Modern and Expressive Language

Rust is a relatively new language, but it has rapidly gained popularity due to its focus on ergonomics and developer productivity. It offers a clean and expressive syntax, powerful abstractions, and a growing ecosystem of libraries that make network programming more enjoyable and efficient.

Features like pattern matching, algebraic data types, and traits contribute to Rust's expressiveness, allowing you to write concise and readable code. Additionally, Cargo, Rust's built-in package manager, simplifies dependency management and build processes, making it easier to get your projects up and running quickly.

Real-World Examples

Rust is already making waves in the network programming world. Here are a few examples of how Rust is being used in real-world projects:

- Firecracker: Amazon Web Services (AWS) uses Rust to power Firecracker, a lightweight virtualization technology that enables secure and efficient serverless computing.
- Linkerd: Linkerd, a popular service mesh for Kubernetes, is written in Rust, providing high performance and reliability for microservices communication.
- Discord: Discord, a popular chat platform, utilizes Rust for its backend infrastructure, handling millions of concurrent users with ease.

These examples demonstrate that Rust is a production-ready language capable of tackling demanding network programming challenges.

In summary, Rust's unique blend of memory safety, fearless concurrency, performance, and expressiveness makes it an ideal choice for building the next generation of network applications. Whether you're a seasoned network programmer or just starting, Rust empowers you to create robust, efficient, and secure software that pushes the boundaries of what's possible.

1.2 Network Fundamentals

Before we dive into the code, let's brush up on some essential networking concepts. Don't worry, we'll keep it concise and focus on the practical stuff.

Internet Protocol Suite

You see, the internet isn't just a magical cloud where data mysteriously appears. It's a complex network of interconnected computers that rely on a set of rules and standards to communicate effectively. Think of the Internet Protocol Suite (also known as TCP/IP) as the fundamental "language" that enables this communication.

Now, this "language" isn't a single monolithic entity. Instead, it's a layered collection of protocols, each with a specific role to play. This layered approach is crucial because it breaks down the complexities of network communication into manageable chunks, making it easier to understand and implement.

Layers of the TCP/IP Model

The TCP/IP model typically consists of four layers, each building upon the one below it:

1. **Application Layer:** This is where the magic happens for you as a user. It's the layer responsible for the applications and services you interact with directly, such as web browsers, email clients, and file transfer programs. These applications use protocols like HTTP, FTP, and SMTP to exchange data.
2. **Transport Layer:** Think of this as the delivery service of the internet. It takes data from the application layer, splits it into smaller packets, and ensures those packets reach their destination reliably and in the correct order. The two primary protocols at this layer are TCP (Transmission Control Protocol) and UDP (User Datagram Protocol).
3. **Network Layer:** This layer handles the addressing and routing of data packets across different networks. It's like the postal service, ensuring that each packet has the correct "address" (IP address) and finds its way through the maze of interconnected networks to reach its destination. The core protocol at this layer is the Internet Protocol (IP).
4. **Link Layer:** This is the layer closest to the physical hardware, dealing with the transmission of raw data bits over a specific physical medium, such as Ethernet cables or Wi-Fi. It ensures that data is transmitted reliably between directly connected devices.

Key Protocols: TCP and UDP

Let's take a closer look at the two workhorses of the transport layer: TCP and UDP.

TCP (Transmission Control Protocol)

TCP is all about reliability. It provides a connection-oriented service, meaning that a connection is established between the sender and receiver before data is transmitted. This connection acts like a dedicated pipeline, ensuring that data arrives in order and without loss.

Here's a simplified analogy: imagine you're sending a fragile package across the country. You'd probably want to use a courier service that provides tracking, insurance, and a guarantee that the package will arrive intact. That's essentially what TCP does for data.

Key features of TCP:

- Connection-oriented: Establishes a connection before data transfer.
- Reliable: Ensures data arrives in order and without loss.
- Flow control: Manages the rate of data transmission to prevent overwhelming the receiver.
- Congestion control: Adjusts the transmission rate to avoid network congestion.

UDP (User Datagram Protocol)

UDP, on the other hand, is like sending a postcard. You drop it in the mailbox, and it hopefully reaches its destination, but there's no guarantee. UDP is a connectionless protocol, meaning there's no initial handshake or ongoing connection between the sender and receiver. It simply fires off data packets without any guarantee of delivery or order.

This might seem unreliable, but UDP has its advantages. It's lightweight and efficient, making it suitable for applications where occasional data loss is acceptable, such as video streaming and online games. In these cases, a brief interruption or a missing frame is less critical than the overall speed and responsiveness.

Key features of UDP:

- Connectionless: No connection establishment required.
- Unreliable: No guarantee of delivery or order.
- Lightweight: Low overhead and minimal processing.
- Fast: Suitable for applications where speed is paramount.

IP Addresses and Ports

To deliver data to the right destination, the Internet Protocol (IP) uses IP addresses. An IP address is like a unique identifier for a device on a network. Think of it as the street address of a house.

But just like a house can have multiple apartments, a device can have multiple applications running simultaneously. To distinguish between these applications, we use ports. A port is like an apartment number within a building, specifying which application should receive the incoming data.

Real-World Examples

The Internet Protocol Suite is the foundation of countless applications and services we use every day. Here are a few examples:

- Web browsing: When you visit a website, your browser uses HTTP (over TCP) to request the web page from the server.
- Email: Sending and receiving emails relies on protocols like SMTP (for sending) and IMAP or POP3 (for receiving).
- File transfer: FTP (File Transfer Protocol) allows you to transfer files between computers.
- Video streaming: Services like Netflix and YouTube use streaming protocols (often based on UDP) to deliver video content.
- Online gaming: Many online games use UDP for real-time communication due to its speed and low latency.

Understanding the Internet Protocol Suite is crucial for anyone working with network applications. It provides the framework for how data is transmitted, addressed, and routed across the internet. In the next section, we'll explore the client-server model, a common architecture for network applications.

Client-Server Model

Now that we've explored the underlying communication framework of the internet, let's talk about how network applications are typically structured. One of the most prevalent architectural patterns in network programming is the client-server model. It's a fundamental concept that you'll encounter throughout your journey in building network applications.

In essence, the client-server model describes a relationship between two processes: the client and the server. Think of it as a conversation where one party initiates the dialogue and the other responds.

- The Client: This is the process that initiates the communication. It sends a request to the server, asking for a specific service or resource. Think of yourself browsing the web: your web browser is the client, sending requests to web servers for web pages.
- The Server: This is the process that listens for incoming requests from clients. It processes these requests and sends back appropriate responses. In our web browsing example, the web server receives your browser's request, fetches the requested web page from its storage, and sends it back to your browser.

How It Works

The interaction between a client and a server typically follows these steps:

1. The client initiates a connection: The client sends a request to the server, specifying the desired service and any necessary data. This request is like a letter addressed to the server, containing the client's wishes.
2. The server listens for connections: The server constantly monitors a specific network address (IP address and port) for incoming client requests. It's like having a receptionist waiting for incoming calls.

3. The server accepts the connection: When the server receives a client request, it establishes a connection with the client, creating a dedicated communication channel between them. This is like the receptionist connecting the caller to the appropriate person.
4. The server processes the request: Once the connection is established, the server receives the client's request and processes it. This might involve accessing a database, performing calculations, or retrieving information from other sources. It's like the person on the other end of the line fulfilling the caller's request.
5. The server sends a response: After processing the request, the server sends a response back to the client. This response contains the requested information or a status indicating the outcome of the request. It's like the person on the phone providing the caller with the information they need.
6. The connection is closed (optional): Depending on the protocol and the nature of the application, the connection may be closed after the response is sent, or it may remain open for further interactions.

Characteristics of the Client-Server Model

The client-server model has several key characteristics that make it suitable for a wide range of network applications:

- Centralized Resources: The server typically manages shared resources, such as data, files, or processing power. This allows clients to access these resources in a controlled and consistent manner.
- Asymmetrical Relationship: The client initiates the communication, and the server responds. This clear division of roles simplifies the design and implementation of network applications.

- Scalability: The client-server model can be scaled to handle a large number of clients by adding more servers or distributing the load across multiple servers.
- Maintainability: Since the server handles the core logic and data, updates and maintenance can be performed centrally without affecting the clients.

Real-World Examples

The client-server model is pervasive in the digital world. Here are a few examples of where you encounter it every day:

- Web browsing: Your web browser (client) requests web pages from web servers.
- Email: Email clients (clients) communicate with mail servers to send and receive emails.
- File sharing: File sharing services use a client-server architecture to allow users to upload and download files.
- Online banking: Banking applications (clients) interact with bank servers to access account information and perform transactions.
- Cloud computing: Cloud services provide resources like storage and computing power through a client-server model.

Code Example: A Simple Echo Server

Let's illustrate the client-server model with a simple code example in Rust. We'll create an "echo server" that receives messages from a client and sends them back.

Rust

```rust
use std::io::{Read, Write};

use std::net::{TcpListener, TcpStream};
```

```rust
use std::thread;

fn handle_client(mut stream: TcpStream) {
    let mut buffer = [0; 1024];
    loop {
        match stream.read(&mut buffer) {
            Ok(0)[1] => break, // Connection closed
            Ok(n) => {

stream.write(&buffer[..n]).unwrap();

            }
            Err(e) => {
                println!("Error: {}", e);
                break;
            }
        }
    }
}
fn main() {
    let listener =
TcpListener::bind("127.0.0.1:8080").unwrap();
    println!("Server listening on port 8080");
```

```
    for stream in listener.incoming() {
        match stream {
            Ok(stream)² => {
                thread::spawn(move || {
                    handle_client(stream);
                });
            }
            Err(e) => {
                println!("Error:³ {}", e);
            }
        }
    }
}
```

In this example, the main function creates a TCP listener that binds to a specific address (127.0.0.1:8080). The incoming() method accepts incoming connections, and for each connection, it spawns a new thread to handle the client communication. The handle_client function reads data from the client and echoes it back.

This is a basic example, but it demonstrates the core principles of the client-server model. As we progress through the book, we'll build more sophisticated network applications using this fundamental pattern.

Common Network Protocols

We've already touched on the foundational protocols of the internet, TCP and UDP, which operate at the transport layer. But the world of network communication is vast and diverse, with a multitude of protocols working together to enable the applications and services we use daily. Think of these protocols as specialized languages spoken by different parts of the network to accomplish specific tasks.

In this section, we'll explore some of the most common network protocols you're likely to encounter in your network programming adventures.

HTTP (Hypertext Transfer Protocol)

HTTP is the undisputed king of the web. It's the protocol that powers the exchange of information between your web browser and web servers, enabling you to access websites, download files, and interact with online services.

HTTP is an application layer protocol, meaning it sits atop the transport layer (usually TCP) and provides a standardized way for clients (like your browser) to request resources from servers and for servers to respond to those requests.

Here's a simplified breakdown of how HTTP works:

1. Request: Your browser sends an HTTP request to a web server, specifying the desired resource (e.g., a web page, an image, a video) and the method of access (e.g., GET, POST, PUT, DELETE).
2. Response: The web server receives the request, processes it, and sends back an HTTP response. The response contains the requested resource (if successful) or an error message (if something went wrong).

HTTP messages are formatted as plain text, making them human-readable and easy to understand. They consist of headers (metadata about the message) and a body (the actual content being transferred).

Real-world examples:

- Browsing a website: When you type a URL into your browser, it uses HTTP to fetch the web page from the corresponding web server.
- Submitting a form: When you fill out a form online, your browser uses HTTP POST request to send the form data to the server.
- Downloading a file: HTTP is used to download files from the internet, such as software updates, documents, and media.
- Accessing APIs: Many web services expose APIs (Application Programming Interfaces) that allow applications to interact with them using HTTP requests.

FTP (File Transfer Protocol)

FTP is the go-to protocol for transferring files between computers on a network. It's like a digital courier service, allowing you to upload files to a server or download files from a server.

FTP operates at the application layer and typically uses TCP as the underlying transport protocol. It establishes two connections between the client and server: one for control commands (e.g., login, directory navigation) and another for data transfer.

Real-world examples:

- Uploading files to a web server: Web developers often use FTP to upload website files to their web hosting server.

- Downloading software updates: Software applications may use FTP to download updates and patches from a central server.
- Sharing files with colleagues: FTP can be used to share files within an organization or with external partners.

SMTP (Simple Mail Transfer Protocol)

SMTP is the protocol that makes email possible. It's responsible for sending emails from your email client to a mail server and for relaying emails between mail servers.

SMTP operates at the application layer and typically uses TCP as the underlying transport protocol. It defines a set of commands for sending email messages, including sender and recipient information, subject line, and message body.

Real-world examples:

- Sending an email from your email client: When you compose and send an email, your email client uses SMTP to send the message to your mail server.
- Receiving an email: While SMTP is used for sending emails, other protocols like IMAP (Internet Message Access Protocol) or POP3 (Post Office Protocol version 3) are used for retrieving emails from a mail server.

DNS (Domain Name System)

DNS is the internet's phonebook. It translates human-readable domain names (like example.com) into numerical IP addresses that computers understand. This is essential because computers rely on IP addresses to locate and communicate with each other on the network.

DNS operates as a distributed database, with servers located throughout the internet. When you type a domain name into your browser, your computer contacts a DNS server to resolve the corresponding IP address.

Real-world examples:

- Accessing a website: Your browser uses DNS to find the IP address of the web server hosting the website you want to visit.
- Sending an email: Your email client uses DNS to find the IP address of the mail server associated with the recipient's email address.
- Using any internet service: DNS is involved in virtually every internet interaction, as it provides the necessary address translation for computers to connect.

Other Common Protocols

Besides the protocols mentioned above, there are countless other protocols that play vital roles in the network ecosystem. Here are a few more you might encounter:

- SSH (Secure Shell): Provides secure remote access to computers.
- TLS/SSL (Transport Layer Security/Secure Sockets Layer): Secures communication by encrypting data transmitted over a network.
- DHCP (Dynamic Host Configuration Protocol): Automatically assigns IP addresses to devices on a network.
- ICMP (Internet Control Message Protocol): Used for network diagnostics and error reporting (e.g., ping).

As you continue your exploration of network programming, you'll undoubtedly encounter more of these specialized protocols. Understanding their purpose and how they interact is crucial for building robust and functional network applications.

1.3 Setting Up Your Environment

Before we embark on our coding adventures, let's ensure you have a comfortable and functional workspace for building Rust network applications. Think of it as setting up your workshop with all the necessary tools and equipment before starting a crafting project.

1.3.1 Installing Rust

The heart of our development environment is the Rust programming language itself. Thankfully, the Rust community has made the installation process quite straightforward, thanks to a handy tool called rustup.

rustup is the official Rust installer and version management tool. It allows you to easily install and update Rust, switch between different versions (stable, beta, nightly), and manage components like the Rust compiler (rustc), the build tool (cargo), and the standard library.

Here's how you can install Rust using rustup:

1. Visit the official Rust website: Open your web browser and navigate to the official Rust website at https://www.rust-lang.org/.
2. Follow the installation instructions: On the website, you'll find clear and concise instructions for installing Rust using rustup on various operating systems (Windows, macOS, Linux). Simply follow the steps provided for your specific platform.
3. Verify the installation: Once the installation is complete, open a terminal or command prompt and type the following command:

Bash

```
rustc --version
```

This command should display the version of the Rust compiler you just installed. If you see the version number, congratulations! You've successfully installed Rust.

1.3.2 Choosing a Code Editor or IDE

Now that you have Rust installed, you'll need a code editor or an Integrated Development Environment (IDE) to write and edit your Rust code. While you can technically use any text editor, some are better suited for Rust development than others, offering features like syntax highlighting, code completion, and debugging support.

Here are a few popular choices:

- VS Code with Rust Analyzer: Visual Studio Code (VS Code) is a free, open-source, and lightweight code editor with a vast ecosystem of extensions. The Rust Analyzer extension provides excellent support for Rust, including code completion, error highlighting, and refactoring tools.
- IntelliJ IDEA with the Rust plugin: IntelliJ IDEA is a powerful IDE known for its robust features and excellent support for various programming languages. The Rust plugin brings similar functionality to IntelliJ IDEA, making it a great choice for Rust development.
- **Vim with rust.vim:** Vim is a highly configurable text editor beloved by many developers for its efficiency and customizability. The rust.vim plugin adds Rust-specific features to Vim, making it a powerful tool for Rustaceans.

Ultimately, the choice of editor or IDE is a matter of personal preference. Experiment with different options and choose the one that best suits your workflow and preferences.

1.3.3 Managing Dependencies with Cargo

Rust has a built-in package manager called Cargo that simplifies the process of managing dependencies in your projects. Cargo allows you to easily add, update, and remove external libraries (crates) that your project relies on.

Here's a quick overview of how Cargo works:

1. **Creating a new project:** To start a new Rust project, open a terminal and use the following command:

Bash

```
cargo new my_project
```

This will create a new directory named my_project with the basic structure for a Rust project, including a Cargo.toml file to manage dependencies.

2. **Adding dependencies:** To add an external crate to your project, open the Cargo.toml file and add the crate name and version under the [dependencies] section. For example, to add the serde crate for serialization, you would add the following line:

Ini, TOML

```
[dependencies]

serde = "1.0"
```

3. **Building and running your project:** To build your project and its dependencies, use the following command:

Bash

```
cargo build
```

To run your project, use:

```Bash
cargo run
```

Cargo will automatically download and compile the necessary crates, making it easy to incorporate external libraries into your Rust projects.

1.3.4 Exploring the Rust Ecosystem

Beyond the core Rust language and tools, a vibrant ecosystem of libraries and resources can aid in your network programming endeavors. Here are a few notable ones:

- Tokio: A powerful asynchronous runtime for Rust, providing the foundation for building high-performance network applications.
- Hyper: A fast and robust HTTP library, ideal for creating web servers and clients.
- Reqwest: An ergonomic HTTP client for making requests to web services.
- Serde: A framework for serializing and deserializing data in various formats, such as JSON, XML, and YAML.

We'll explore these libraries in more detail throughout the book as we build different network applications.

With your Rust environment set up and your tools ready, you're well-equipped to begin your journey into the exciting world of Rust network programming. Let's move on to Chapter 2, where we'll lay the groundwork with essential Rust concepts.

Chapter 2: Rust Essentials for Networking

This chapter will equip you with the essential Rust knowledge you'll need to confidently tackle network programming challenges. We'll explore how Rust handles data, how it deals with those pesky errors (because let's face it, they happen!), and how its unique approach to memory management makes your network applications safer and more reliable. And finally, we'll take our first steps into the exciting world of concurrency with threads.

2.1 Working with Data

Just like any programming language, Rust provides various ways to represent and manipulate data. But Rust has a few tricks up its sleeve that make it particularly well-suited for network programming. Let's explore some of the key data types and structures you'll be working with.

2.1.1 Primitive Data Types

Let's talk about the fundamental building blocks of data in Rust: primitive data types. These are the basic types that the language provides out of the box, and they form the foundation for more complex data structures. Think of them as the essential ingredients in your network programming recipe book.

Integers

Integers are your bread and butter when it comes to representing whole numbers. You'll use them for things like counting network packets, storing port numbers, and representing sizes of data buffers. Rust offers a variety of integer types to cater to different needs and memory constraints:

- Signed Integers: These can represent both positive and negative numbers. The most common ones you'll encounter are:
    - i8: 8-bit signed integer (range: -128 to 127)
    - i16: 16-bit signed integer (range: -32,768 to 32,767)
    - i32: 32-bit signed integer (range: -2,147,483,648 to 2,147,483,647)
    - i64: 64-bit signed integer (range: -9,223,372,036,854,775,808 to 9,223,372,036,854,775,807)
    - isize: Signed integer with a size dependent on the architecture (32-bit on 32-bit systems, 64-bit on 64-bit systems)
- Unsigned Integers: These represent only non-negative numbers (0 and positive numbers). Their counterparts are:
    - u8: 8-bit unsigned integer (range: 0 to 255)
    - u16: 16-bit unsigned integer (range: 0 to 65,535)
    - u32: 32-bit unsigned integer (range: 0 to 4,294,967,295)
    - u64: 64-bit unsigned integer (range: 0 to 18,446,744,073,709,551,615)
    - usize: Unsigned integer with a size dependent on the architecture

Choosing the right integer type depends on the range of values you need to represent and the memory efficiency you desire. For instance, if you're storing a port number (which ranges from 0 to 65,535), a u16 would be a suitable choice.

Floating-Point Numbers

When you need to work with numbers that have fractional parts, like 3.14 or -2.718, floating-point numbers are your friends. Rust provides two primary floating-point types:

- f32: Single-precision floating-point number (32 bits)

- f64: Double-precision floating-point number (64 bits)

Double-precision numbers offer greater precision and a wider range of values, but they also consume more memory. You might use floating-point numbers for calculations involving network timings, data analysis, or scientific computations within your network applications.

Booleans

Booleans are the simplest data type, representing only two possible values: true or false. They're essential for controlling program flow, making decisions, and representing binary states.

You'll often use booleans in conditional statements, like this:

```Rust
let connected = true;

if connected {
    println!("The connection is established.");
} else {
    println!("No connection found.");
}
```

In this example, the connected variable holds a boolean value, and the if statement executes different code blocks depending on whether the value is true or false.

Characters

Characters represent single Unicode characters, such as letters, numbers, symbols, and even emojis. They're essential for working with text-based protocols and data formats like HTTP and XML.

In Rust, characters are enclosed in single quotes, like 'a' or '?'. You can use them to build strings, analyze text data, and interact with user input.

Working with Primitive Data Types

Here's a simple example that demonstrates how you might use primitive data types in a network-related context:

```Rust
fn main() {
    let port: u16 = 8080; // Port number

    let address = "127.0.0.1"; // IP address

    let is_connected: bool = true; // Connection status

    println!("Connecting to {}:{}...", address, port);

    if is_connected {
        println!("Connection successful!");
    }
}
```

In this example, we use a u16 to store the port number, a string (&str) to store the IP address, and a boolean to represent the connection status.

Understanding these primitive data types is crucial for working with data in Rust. They form the basis for more complex data structures and are essential for building robust and efficient network applications. As we move forward, we'll explore how to combine these basic types to create more sophisticated data representations.

2.1.2 Strings and Byte Arrays

When it comes to network programming, you're constantly dealing with sequences of bytes. These bytes might represent human-readable text, like an HTTP request, or raw binary data, like an image file. Rust provides two primary ways to handle these sequences: strings and byte arrays. Let's explore each of them in detail.

Strings (String**)**

Strings in Rust are designed to handle text. They're sequences of Unicode characters, which means they can represent text in various languages and include special characters like emojis. Rust's String type is dynamic and flexible, allowing you to modify the string's content and size as needed.

Here are some key characteristics of Rust strings:

- UTF-8 encoded: Rust strings are stored using the UTF-8 encoding, a universal character encoding that can represent a wide range of characters from different languages.
- Mutable: You can modify the contents of a String after it's created. You can append characters, remove characters, or replace substrings.
- Owned: A String owns the memory it uses to store the text data. This means that when a String goes out of scope, the memory is automatically deallocated.
- Heap-allocated: The text data of a String is stored on the heap, a region of memory used for dynamically allocated data. This allows strings to grow or shrink as needed.

Here are some common ways to create and manipulate strings in Rust:

Rust

```rust
let mut message = String::from("Hello"); // Create a string from a literal

message.push_str(", world!"); // Append to the string

println!("{}", message); // Output: Hello, world!

let greeting = String::new(); // Create an empty string

let name = "Alice";

let personalized_greeting = format!("Hello, {}!", name); // Format a string

println!("{}", personalized_greeting); // Output: Hello, Alice!
```

Byte Arrays ([u8])

While strings are great for text, sometimes you need to work with raw bytes without any assumptions about character encoding. That's where byte arrays come in.

A byte array is a fixed-size sequence of bytes (u8). It's like a container that holds a specific number of bytes. You can access individual bytes in the array using indexing, and you can modify the bytes directly.

Here are some key characteristics of byte arrays:

- Fixed-size: A byte array has a fixed size determined at compile time. You can't change the size of the array after it's created.

- Stack-allocated: Byte arrays are typically allocated on the stack, a region of memory used for statically allocated data. This makes them efficient for small, fixed-size data.
- Mutable: You can modify the individual bytes within a byte array.

Here's an example of how you might use a byte array to store and manipulate binary data:

Rust

let mut buffer = [0; 1024]; // Create a byte array of size 1024

// Fill the buffer with some data...

buffer[0] = 10; // Modify the first byte

buffer[1] = 20; // Modify the second byte

// Process the data in the buffer...

Strings vs. Byte Arrays in Network Programming

So, when should you use strings versus byte arrays in network programming? Here's a general guideline:

Use strings when:

- You're dealing with text-based protocols like HTTP, FTP, or SMTP.
- You need to manipulate or analyze text data.
- You need a flexible data structure that can grow or shrink as needed.

Use byte arrays when:

- You're dealing with raw binary data, like image files or network packets.
- You need a fixed-size buffer to store data received from a network connection.
- You need direct access to individual bytes for manipulation or analysis.

Real-World Examples

- HTTP Requests and Responses: HTTP messages are typically represented as strings because they contain text-based headers and often have text-based content (like HTML).
- Network Packet Headers: Network packet headers often contain binary data, such as source and destination addresses, packet types, and checksums. Byte arrays are well-suited for representing this data.
- File Transfer: When transferring files over a network, you might use byte arrays to buffer the data being read from or written to the file.
- Cryptography: Cryptographic operations often involve manipulating raw bytes, making byte arrays a common choice for handling cryptographic keys and ciphertext.

Understanding the strengths and weaknesses of strings and byte arrays is crucial for writing efficient and reliable network applications in Rust. Choose the right data structure for the task at hand, and you'll be well-equipped to handle the diverse data you'll encounter in the network world.

2.1.3 Structs and Enums

Alright, let's move beyond the basic data types and explore how Rust allows you to create your own custom data structures. This is where things get really interesting, as you can start modeling the data in your network applications in a way that makes sense for your specific needs.

Think of structs and enums as blueprints for creating complex data types tailored to your network programming tasks. They're like specialized containers that hold related pieces of information together in an organized way.

Structs

Structs are like blueprints for creating custom data types that group related pieces of information together. They're incredibly useful for representing complex data structures in your network applications.

Imagine you're working with network packets. Each packet might have a source address, a destination address, a sequence number, and a payload of data. Instead of juggling these individual pieces of information separately, you can create a Packet struct to bundle them together:

Rust

```rust
struct Packet {
    source_address: String,
    destination_address: String,
    sequence_number: u32,
    payload: Vec<u8>,
}
```

This Packet struct acts as a blueprint for creating packet objects. Each packet object will have its own values for source_address, destination_address, sequence_number, and payload.

Here's how you might create and use a Packet object:

```rust
let packet = Packet {
    source_address: String::from("192.168.1.10"),
    destination_address: String::from("192.168.1.20"),
    sequence_number: 12345,
    payload: vec![10, 20, 30, 40, 50],
};

println!("Packet source: {}", packet.source_address);

println!("Packet destination: {}", packet.destination_address);
```

This creates a packet object with the specified values and then accesses its fields using dot notation (e.g., packet.source_address).

Structs are incredibly versatile. You can use them to represent all sorts of data in your network applications, such as:

- Network messages: Define structs to represent the structure of messages exchanged between clients and servers.
- Configuration settings: Store configuration parameters for your network applications in a struct.
- Data records: Represent data retrieved from a database or a network service as structs.

Enums

Enums, short for enumerations, are another powerful tool for defining custom data types. They allow you to define a type that can have one of several named values.

For example, imagine you're building a network application that supports different types of requests, such as "GET", "POST", "PUT", and "DELETE". You could represent these request types using an enum:

Rust

```rust
enum RequestType {
    Get,
    Post,
    Put,
    Delete,
}
```

This RequestType enum defines four possible values: Get, Post, Put, and Delete. You can then use this enum to represent the type of a request in your code:

Rust

```rust
let request_type = RequestType::Get;

match request_type {
    RequestType::Get => {
        // Handle a GET request
    }
```

```
    RequestType::Post => {

        // Handle a POST request

    }

    // ... handle other request types

}
```

This code snippet uses a match expression to perform different actions based on the value of request_type.

Enums are particularly useful when you have a fixed set of possible values for a variable. They provide type safety and make your code more readable by giving meaningful names to these values.

Here are some other ways you might use enums in network programming:

- Protocol versions: Represent different versions of a network protocol (e.g., HTTP/1.1, HTTP/2).
- Connection states: Represent the different states of a network connection (e.g., Connecting, Connected, Disconnected).
- Error types: Define specific error types that your network application might encounter.

Combining Structs and Enums

You can even combine structs and enums to create more complex and expressive data structures. For example, you might define a struct to represent a network message that includes a field indicating the message type using an enum:

Rust

```
enum MessageType {
```

```
    Request,

    Response,

}

struct NetworkMessage {

    message_type: MessageType,

    payload: Vec<u8>,

}
```

This `NetworkMessage` struct can now represent both requests and responses, with the `message_type` field indicating the specific type.

Structs and enums are essential tools for organizing and structuring your data in Rust. They allow you to create custom data types that accurately model the information you're working with in your network applications. As you become more comfortable with Rust, you'll find yourself using them extensively to build elegant and maintainable code.

2.2 Error Handling

Let's face it, in the world of network programming, things don't always go smoothly. Network connections can drop, data can get corrupted, servers can become unavailable, and unexpected situations can arise. That's why robust error handling is absolutely crucial for building reliable and resilient network applications.

Rust takes a unique and powerful approach to error handling that helps you write code that is not only correct but also easy to understand and maintain. Let's explore how Rust's error handling mechanisms can make your network programming life easier.

The Result Type

At the heart of Rust's error handling is the Result type. Think of it as a container that holds the outcome of an operation that might fail. It can have two possible states:

- Ok(T): This indicates that the operation was successful, and the Ok variant holds the resulting value of type T.
- Err(E): This indicates that the operation failed, and the Err variant holds an error value of type E.

Many functions in Rust's standard library and network-related crates return Result types to signal potential errors. For example, the TcpStream::connect() function, which we've seen before, returns a Result<TcpStream, std::io::Error>:

Rust

```rust
use std::net::TcpStream;

let result = TcpStream::connect("127.0.0.1:8080");
```

This means that result can either be Ok(TcpStream) if the connection is successful, or Err(std::io::Error) if an error occurs during the connection attempt.

Handling Results

Rust provides several ways to handle Result values and deal with potential errors:

- match **Expression:** This allows you to exhaustively handle both the Ok and Err cases:

Rust

```rust
match result {
```

```
    Ok(stream) => {

        println!("Connected to the server!");

        // Do something with the stream

    }

    Err(e) => {

        println!("Failed to connect: {}", e);

        // Handle the error appropriately

    }

}
```

- unwrap() **Method:** This method is a shortcut for extracting the value from an Ok result. If the result is Err, it will panic and terminate the program. Use this with caution, mainly for prototyping or when you're absolutely certain an error won't occur.

Rust

```
let stream = result.unwrap(); // Panics if result is Err
```

- expect() **Method:** Similar to unwrap(), but allows you to provide a custom panic message:

Rust

```
let stream = result.expect("Failed to connect to the server");
```

- **? Operator:** This operator is a concise way to propagate errors up the call stack. If the result is Ok, it extracts the value. If the result is Err, it returns the error from the current function.

```Rust
fn connect_to_server() -> Result<TcpStream, std::io::Error> {
    let stream = TcpStream::connect("127.0.0.1:8080")?; // Propagate error if connection fails
    Ok(stream)
}
```

Defining Custom Error Types

While Rust provides many built-in error types, you can also define your own custom error types to represent specific errors that might occur in your network applications. This allows you to provide more informative error messages and handle different error scenarios more effectively.

Here's an example of how you might define a custom error type:

```Rust
use std::error::Error;

use std::fmt;

#[derive(Debug)]

struct NetworkError {
    message: String,
```

```rust
}

impl fmt::Display for NetworkError {
    fn fmt(&self, f: &mut fmt::Formatter) -> fmt::Result {
        write!(f,[1] "Network error: {}", self.message)
    }
}

impl Error for NetworkError {}

// Example usage

fn connect_to_server() -> Result<(), NetworkError> {
    // ... attempt to connect to the server ...
    if connection_failed {
        return Err(NetworkError { message: String::from("Connection refused") });
    }
    Ok(())
}
```

In this example, we define a NetworkError struct that holds a message describing the error. We implement the Display and Error traits to allow our custom error type to be formatted and used with the ? operator.

Real-World Examples

Error handling is crucial in virtually every network application. Here are a few real-world scenarios where proper error handling is essential:

- Handling connection failures: When attempting to connect to a remote server, the connection might fail due to various reasons (e.g., server unavailable, network issues). Your application should gracefully handle these failures, perhaps by retrying the connection or displaying an informative error message to the user.
- Dealing with corrupted data: Network data can sometimes be corrupted during transmission. Your application should be able to detect and handle corrupted data, perhaps by requesting retransmission or discarding the invalid data.
- Managing timeouts: Network operations can sometimes take longer than expected. Your application should implement timeouts to prevent indefinite waiting and handle potential timeout errors.

By embracing Rust's error handling mechanisms and employing best practices, you can build robust and reliable network applications that gracefully handle the inevitable hiccups that occur in the network world.

2.3 Memory Management and Ownership

One of the things that makes Rust truly stand out from other languages is its unique approach to memory management. This is where Rust's superpowers of memory safety and performance really shine. It's a bit different from what you might be used to in languages like C or Java, but trust me, it's worth understanding.

Ownership

The core idea behind Rust's memory management is *ownership*. Think of it like this: every value in Rust has a single owner at any given time. It's like having the sole key to a safe deposit box – only the key holder can access what's inside.

When the owner goes out of scope, the value is automatically dropped, and the associated memory is freed. It's like returning the key to the bank, and the contents of the box are no longer accessible.

This simple rule has profound implications:

- No Memory Leaks: Since every value has an owner responsible for cleaning it up, you avoid memory leaks, where memory is allocated but never freed. This is crucial in long-running network applications that need to stay stable and efficient.
- No Dangling Pointers: Dangling pointers are a notorious source of bugs in languages like C. They occur when you have a pointer to a memory location that has been freed. Rust's ownership system prevents this by ensuring that a value can't be accessed after its owner goes out of scope.
- No Data Races: Data races happen when multiple threads access and modify the same data concurrently without proper synchronization. Rust's ownership rules prevent data races at compile time, making your concurrent network applications safer and more reliable.

Borrowing

While ownership provides strong safety guarantees, sometimes you need to share access to a value without transferring ownership. That's where *borrowing* comes in.

Borrowing allows you to temporarily access a value without taking ownership. It's like borrowing a book from a library – you can read it, but you have to return it eventually.

Rust has two types of borrows:

- Immutable Borrows (&T): These allow you to read a value but not modify it. It's like borrowing a book for reference – you can read it, but you can't write in it.
- Mutable Borrows (&mut T): These allow you to both read and modify a value. It's like borrowing a book to take notes – you can both read and write in it.

Rust enforces strict rules for borrowing to ensure memory safety:

- You can have multiple immutable borrows of a value at the same time. It's like multiple people reading the same book simultaneously.
- You can have only one mutable borrow of a value at a time. It's like only one person being allowed to borrow a book for taking notes at any given time.
- You cannot have both mutable and immutable borrows of a value at the same time. It's like not allowing someone to write in a book while others are reading it.

These rules might seem restrictive at first, but they prevent common concurrency bugs and ensure that your network applications are free from data races and memory corruption.

Real-World Examples

Let's see how ownership and borrowing apply to real-world network programming scenarios:

- Passing Data to Functions: When you pass data to a function in Rust, you're essentially lending that data to the

function for the duration of its execution. The function can borrow the data immutable or mutable, depending on whether it needs to modify it.
- Sharing Data Between Threads: When you share data between threads, you need to ensure that the data is accessed safely to avoid data races. Rust's ownership and borrowing rules help you achieve this by enforcing strict access control.
- Managing Network Connections: When you establish a network connection, you typically obtain a handle to the connection (e.g., a TcpStream). This handle represents ownership of the connection. When the handle goes out of scope, the connection is automatically closed.

Code Example

Here's a simple example that demonstrates ownership and borrowing in Rust:

Rust

```rust
fn main() {
    let s1 = String::from("hello"); // s1 owns the string

    let len = calculate_length(&s1); // Pass an immutable borrow of s1

    println!("The length of '{}' is {}.", s1, len);

}

fn calculate_length(s: &String) -> usize { // s immutably borrows the string
    s.len()
```

}

In this example, the calculate_length function borrows the string s1 immutably. This allows the function to access the string without taking ownership, and s1 remains valid after the function call.

Rust's ownership and borrowing system might take some getting used to, but it's a powerful tool that ensures memory safety and prevents common pitfalls in network programming. By understanding these concepts, you'll be well-equipped to write robust and efficient network applications in Rust.

2.4 Introduction to Concurrency with Threads

In network programming, it's often essential to handle multiple tasks seemingly at the same time. You might need to process incoming connections from multiple clients, send data over the network, and perform background operations, all while keeping your application responsive. This is where concurrency comes into play, and Rust offers powerful tools to tackle it effectively.

One of the fundamental ways to achieve concurrency in Rust is through threads. Think of a thread as a lightweight, independent worker within your application. Each thread can execute its own set of instructions concurrently with other threads, allowing your application to perform multiple tasks seemingly simultaneously.

Creating Threads

Rust provides a straightforward way to create threads using the std::thread module. The thread::spawn() function creates a new thread and executes the provided code within that thread.

Here's a simple example:

Rust

```rust
use std::thread;

use std::time::Duration;

fn main() {
    thread::spawn(|| {
        for i in 1..5 {
            println!("Hello from spawned thread! {}", i);

            thread::sleep(Duration::from_millis(100));
        }
    });

    for i in 1..5 {
        println!("Hello from main thread! {}", i);

        thread::sleep(Duration::from_millis(100));
    }
}
```

In this example, we create a new thread using thread::spawn(). The code within the closure (the || { ... } block) will be executed in the new thread. Both the main thread and the spawned thread will print their messages concurrently, resulting in interleaved output.

Waiting for Threads

Sometimes, you need to wait for a thread to finish its execution before proceeding. The join() method allows you to do just that. It blocks the current thread until the joined thread has completed.

Here's how you can use join():

Rust

```
use std::thread;

fn main() {

    let handle = thread::spawn(|| {

        // ... some code to execute in the thread ...

    });

    handle.join().unwrap(); // Wait for the thread to finish

    // ... code to execute after the thread has finished ...

}
```

In this example, the handle.join().unwrap() line will block the main thread until the spawned thread completes its execution.

Sharing Data Between Threads

Sharing data between threads requires careful consideration to avoid data races and other concurrency-related issues. Rust's ownership and borrowing rules, along with synchronization primitives like mutexes, help you manage shared data safely.

We'll explore these concepts in more detail in later chapters when we discuss advanced concurrency patterns.

Real-World Examples

Threads are invaluable in network programming for various tasks:

- Handling Multiple Clients: A web server can use threads to handle requests from multiple clients concurrently. Each thread can be dedicated to serving a specific client, ensuring responsiveness even under heavy load.
- Performing Background Tasks: You might use threads to perform background operations, such as downloading files, processing data, or interacting with external services, without blocking the main thread.
- Improving Performance: Threads can be used to parallelize computationally intensive tasks, such as data encryption or compression, potentially improving the performance of your network applications.

While threads are powerful, they also introduce complexities. Managing shared data, avoiding deadlocks, and ensuring proper synchronization require careful design and implementation. As we progress through the book, we'll explore more advanced concurrency patterns and techniques that can help you tackle these challenges effectively.

Chapter 3: Sockets and Low-Level Networking

Think of sockets as the doorways through which your Rust applications can communicate with the outside world. They provide the fundamental mechanism for sending and receiving data over a network.

In this chapter, we'll explore the std::net module, Rust's built-in library for working with sockets. We'll learn how to create TCP and UDP sockets, how to send and receive data through them, and how to configure them to suit your needs.

3.1 The std::net Module

Think of the std::net module as your interface to the underlying network stack of your operating system. It provides a safe and convenient way to interact with network resources without having to deal with the complexities of system calls and raw sockets.

Representing Network Addresses

Before you can send or receive data over a network, you need a way to identify the participants in the communication. This is where network addresses come in. The std::net module provides types for representing various kinds of network addresses:

- IpAddr: This enum represents an IP address, which can be either IPv4 or IPv6. It's like a universal address format that can accommodate both older and newer versions of the internet protocol.

Rust

```rust
use std::net::IpAddr;
```

```rust
let ipv4_addr =
IpAddr::V4(std::net::Ipv4Addr::new(127, 0, 0,
1));

let ipv6_addr =
IpAddr::V6(std::net::Ipv6Addr::new(0, 0, 0, 0, 0,
0, 0, 1));
```

- **Ipv4Addr:** This struct represents an IPv4 address, the traditional format with four numbers separated by dots (e.g., 192.168.1.1).

Rust

```rust
use std::net::Ipv4Addr;

let local_addr = Ipv4Addr::new(127, 0, 0, 1); // Represents localhost
```

- **Ipv6Addr:** This struct represents an IPv6 address, the newer format with eight groups of hexadecimal numbers separated by colons (e.g., 2001:0db8:85a3:0000:0000:8a2e:0370:7334).

Rust

```rust
use std::net::Ipv6Addr;

let loopback_addr = Ipv6Addr::new(0, 0, 0, 0, 0, 0, 0, 1); // Represents the loopback address
```

- **SocketAddr:** This enum represents a socket address, which combines an IP address and a port number. It's like the complete address of an apartment building, including the street address and the apartment number.

```rust
use std::net::SocketAddr;

let socket_addr: SocketAddr =
"127.0.0.1:8080".parse().unwrap();
```

Working with Sockets

Sockets are the fundamental building blocks for network communication. They provide the interface through which your application can send and receive data over a network. The std::net module offers types for working with different kinds of sockets:

- **TcpListener**: This struct is used for creating TCP servers. It allows you to bind to a specific address and listen for incoming connections from clients.

```rust
use std::net::TcpListener;

let listener =
TcpListener::bind("127.0.0.1:8080").unwrap();
```

- **TcpStream**: This struct represents a TCP connection. It can be used by both clients to connect to a server and by servers to accept connections from clients.

```rust
use std::net::TcpStream;

// Client connecting to a server

let stream =
TcpStream::connect("127.0.0.1:8080").unwrap();
```

```rust
// Server accepting a connection

let (stream, addr) = listener.accept().unwrap();
```

- **UdpSocket:** This struct is used for sending and receiving UDP datagrams. It allows you to bind to an address and send datagrams to specific destinations, as well as receive datagrams from other sources.

Rust

```rust
use std::net::UdpSocket;

let socket = UdpSocket::bind("127.0.0.1:8080").unwrap();
```

Other Useful Types and Functions

The std::net module also provides other useful types and functions for network programming:

- ToSocketAddrs **trait:** This trait allows you to convert various types (e.g., strings, tuples) into SocketAddr objects, making it easier to work with socket addresses.
- Shutdown **enum:** This enum is used to control the shutdown behavior of a TCP stream, allowing you to specify whether to shut down the read half, the write half, or both halves of the connection.
- SocketAddrV4 **and** SocketAddrV6 **structs:** These structs represent socket addresses specifically for IPv4 and IPv6, respectively.

Real-World Examples

The std::net module is used extensively in various network applications:

- Web servers: Web servers use `TcpListener` to listen for incoming HTTP requests from clients.
- Chat applications: Chat applications might use `TcpStream` for persistent connections between clients and a server, or `UdpSocket` for real-time message exchange.
- Game servers: Game servers often use UDP sockets for fast and efficient communication between players and the game server.
- Network tools: Network diagnostic tools like `ping` and `traceroute` use ICMP (Internet Control Message Protocol), which is accessible through the `std::net` module.

Understanding the types and functions provided by the `std::net` module, you gain the foundation for building a wide range of network applications in Rust. It's your gateway to the world of low-level networking, allowing you to create, manage, and interact with sockets effectively.

3.2 TCP Sockets

TCP (Transmission Control Protocol) is the reliable workhorse of the internet. It provides a connection-oriented communication channel, ensuring that data is delivered reliably and in order. Let's see how to work with TCP sockets in Rust.

Creating a TCP Server

Let's dive into the world of TCP servers in Rust! As you may recall, TCP (Transmission Control Protocol) is like the reliable courier service of the internet. It ensures that data is delivered in order and without loss, making it a great choice for applications that demand dependable communication.

Building a TCP server involves a few key steps:

1. Creating a `TcpListener`: This is like setting up a reception desk at your server's address (IP address and port number).

The TcpListener will patiently wait for incoming client connections.
2. **Binding to an Address:** This is like assigning a specific location to your reception desk. You need to tell the TcpListener which IP address and port number it should listen on.
3. **Accepting Connections:** When a client attempts to connect, the TcpListener accepts the connection, establishing a dedicated communication channel between the server and the client. It's like the receptionist welcoming a visitor and guiding them to the appropriate meeting room.
4. **Handling Client Communication:** Once a connection is established, the server can communicate with the client, sending and receiving data. This is where the actual work of your server takes place, whether it's serving web pages, processing requests, or exchanging messages.

Code Example: A Basic TCP Server

Let's put these steps into action with a simple code example:

```rust
Rust

use std::io::{Read, Write};

use std::net::{TcpListener, TcpStream};

use std::thread;

fn handle_client(mut stream: TcpStream) {
    let mut buffer = [0; 1024];

    loop {
        match stream.read(&mut buffer) {
            Ok(0)[1] => break, // Connection closed
```

```rust
            Ok(n) => {


stream.write(&buffer[..n]).unwrap(); // Echo the data back

            }
            Err(e) => {
                println!("Error: {}", e);
                break;
            }
        }
    }
}
fn main() {
    let listener = TcpListener::bind("127.0.0.1:8080").unwrap();
    println!("Server listening on port 8080");
    for stream in listener.incoming() {
        match stream {
            Ok(stream)² => {
                thread::spawn(move || {
                    handle_client(stream);
                });
```

```
            }
            Err(e) => {
                println!("Error: {}", e);
            }
        }
    }
}
```

In this example:

- We create a TcpListener that binds to the local address 127.0.0.1:8080.
- The incoming() method returns an iterator that yields incoming connections as TcpStream objects.
- For each incoming connection, we spawn a new thread to handle the client communication in the handle_client function.
- The handle_client function reads data from the client and echoes it back, effectively creating a simple "echo server."

Real-World Examples

TCP servers are the backbone of countless internet services:

- Web servers: Web servers like Apache and Nginx use TCP to serve web pages and other content to users' browsers.
- Mail servers: Mail servers use TCP to handle email communication, sending and receiving messages between users.
- File servers: File servers use TCP to allow users to upload and download files over a network.

- Game servers: Many online games use TCP for reliable communication between players and the game server.
- Database servers: Database servers use TCP to handle client connections and database queries.

Important Considerations

When building TCP servers, keep these points in mind:

- Error Handling: Network operations can fail, so it's crucial to handle potential errors gracefully. Use Rust's `Result` type and error handling mechanisms to ensure your server can recover from unexpected situations.
- Concurrency: To handle multiple clients efficiently, you'll often need to use concurrency techniques like threads or asynchronous programming. We'll explore these in more detail in later chapters.
- Security: If your server handles sensitive data, you'll need to implement security measures like encryption and authentication to protect it from unauthorized access.

This section has provided a solid foundation for creating TCP servers in Rust. You've learned how to create a `TcpListener`, bind it to an address, accept connections, and handle client communication. With this knowledge, you can start building simple TCP-based network applications. As we progress through the book, we'll explore more advanced techniques for building robust and scalable TCP servers.

Creating a TCP Client

Now that we've explored the server-side of TCP communication, let's shift our focus to the client. In the client-server model, the client is the one who initiates the conversation, reaching out to the server to request a service or retrieve information.

Building a TCP client in Rust involves these key steps:

1. Creating a **TcpStream**: This is like picking up the phone and dialing the server's number. The TcpStream represents the connection between the client and the server.
2. Connecting to the Server: This is like establishing the call with the server. You need to specify the server's address (IP address and port number) to initiate the connection.
3. Sending Data to the Server: Once the connection is established, the client can send data to the server. This could be anything from a simple text message to a complex data structure.
4. Receiving Data from the Server: The client can also receive data from the server. This could be the server's response to the client's request or some other information the server wants to send.

Code Example: A Basic TCP Client

Let's see how to create a simple TCP client in Rust:

```rust
use std::io::{Read, Write};

use std::net::TcpStream;

fn main() {

    let mut stream = TcpStream::connect("127.0.0.1:8080").unwrap();

    println!("Connected to the server");[1]

    stream.write(b"Hello from the client!\n").unwrap();

    let mut buffer = [0; 1024];
```

```rust
    let bytes_read = stream.read(&mut buffer).unwrap();

    println!(
        "Received {} bytes: {}",
        bytes_read,
        String::from_utf8_lossy(&buffer[..bytes_read])
    );
}
```

In this example:

- We create a TcpStream by connecting to the server running on 127.0.0.1:8080.
- We send a message to the server using the write() method.
- We receive data from the server using the read() method and print it to the console.

Real-World Examples

TCP clients are everywhere in the digital world:

- Web browsers: Your web browser is a TCP client that connects to web servers to retrieve web pages and other content.
- Email clients: Email clients use TCP to connect to mail servers to send and receive emails.
- FTP clients: FTP clients use TCP to connect to FTP servers to upload and download files.
- SSH clients: SSH clients use TCP to establish secure connections to remote servers.

- Online game clients: Online game clients use TCP to connect to game servers to participate in multiplayer games.

Important Considerations

When building TCP clients, keep these points in mind:

- Error Handling: Network connections can fail, and data transmission can be interrupted. It's crucial to handle potential errors gracefully using Rust's error handling mechanisms.
- Timeouts: You might want to set timeouts on network operations to prevent your client from waiting indefinitely for a response from the server.
- Security: If you're dealing with sensitive data, you might need to use encryption and authentication to secure the communication between the client and the server.

Sending and Receiving Data

Alright, now that we've established a connection between our client and server using TcpStream, it's time for the real action: exchanging data! This is where the magic of network communication happens, allowing applications to share information and collaborate.

Think of a TcpStream as a two-way communication channel, like a telephone conversation. Both the client and the server can send data to each other through this channel, enabling them to exchange messages, files, or any other kind of information.

Sending Data with write()

To send data through a TcpStream, you use the write() method. This method takes a byte slice (&[u8]) as input and sends those bytes over the network to the other end of the connection.

Rust

```rust
use std::net::TcpStream;

use std::io::Write;

fn main() {

    let mut stream = TcpStream::connect("127.0.0.1:8080").unwrap();

    stream.write(b"Hello from the client!\n").unwrap();

}
```

In this example, we send the message "Hello from the client!\n" to the server. Note that we're sending a byte slice (b"Hello from the client!\n"), as the write() method expects binary data.

Receiving Data with read()

To receive data from a TcpStream, you use the read() method. This method takes a mutable byte slice (&mut [u8]) as input and fills it with the received data.

Rust

```rust
use std::net::TcpStream;

use std::io::Read;

fn main() {

    let mut stream = TcpStream::connect("127.0.0.1:8080").unwrap();

    let mut buffer = [0; 1024];
```

```rust
    let bytes_read = stream.read(&mut buffer).unwrap();

    println!(
        "Received {} bytes: {}",
        bytes_read,
        String::from_utf8_lossy(&buffer[..bytes_read])
    );
}
```

In this example, we create a buffer of 1024 bytes and use the read() method to receive data from the server. The read() method returns the number of bytes read, which we then use to print the received message.

Handling Partial Reads and Writes

It's important to note that read() and write() might not always process all the data you provide in a single call. This can happen due to network conditions or buffer limitations. Therefore, you might need to call these methods repeatedly to ensure that all the data is sent or received.

Rust

```rust
use std::net::TcpStream;

use std::io::Write;

fn main() {
    let mut stream = TcpStream::connect("127.0.0.1:8080").unwrap();
```

```rust
    let message = b"This is a longer message that might not be sent in a single write call.\n";

    let mut bytes_written = 0;

    while bytes_written < message.len() {

        match stream.write(&message[bytes_written..]) {

            Ok(n) => bytes_written += n,

            Err(e) => {

                println!("Error: {}", e);

                break;

            }

        }

    }

}
```

In this example, we use a loop to repeatedly call write() until all the bytes in the message have been sent.

Real-World Examples

Sending and receiving data over TCP connections is the foundation of many internet applications:

- Web browsing: Your web browser sends HTTP requests to web servers and receives HTML, images, and other content in response.
- File transfer: FTP clients send commands to FTP servers and receive files or directory listings in response.

- Chat applications: Chat applications send and receive messages between users over TCP connections.
- Online games: Online games often use TCP to exchange game state information and player actions between clients and the game server.

Important Considerations

When sending and receiving data over TCP, keep these points in mind:

- Data Representation: Ensure that the data you send and receive is in a format that both the client and server understand. This might involve using serialization techniques to convert complex data structures into a byte stream.
- Buffering: Use buffers to efficiently handle data transmission. Buffers can help reduce the number of system calls and improve performance.
- Flow Control: TCP has built-in flow control mechanisms to prevent one side of the connection from overwhelming the other with data. However, you might need to implement additional flow control measures in your application if necessary.

3.3 UDP Sockets

UDP (User Datagram Protocol) is the speed demon of the internet. It provides a connectionless communication channel, sacrificing reliability for speed and efficiency. Let's see how to work with UDP sockets in Rust.

Sending and Receiving Datagrams

Alright, let's switch gears and explore the world of UDP communication in Rust. UDP (User Datagram Protocol) is like sending a postcard – you drop it in the mailbox, and it hopefully reaches its destination, but there's no guarantee. This might sound a bit unreliable, but UDP has its advantages: it's fast, lightweight, and efficient, making it a good choice for applications where occasional data loss is acceptable.

Instead of establishing a persistent connection like TCP, UDP communication involves sending and receiving individual packets of data called datagrams. Each datagram is like a self-contained message with its own source and destination address.

Sending Datagrams with send_to()

To send a datagram using a UDP socket, you use the send_to() method. This method takes two arguments:

- A byte slice (&[u8]) containing the data you want to send.
- The address (SocketAddr) of the recipient.

Rust

```rust
use std::net::{UdpSocket, SocketAddr};

fn main() {
    let socket = UdpSocket::bind("127.0.0.1:8080").unwrap();

    let destination: SocketAddr = "127.0.0.1:8081".parse().unwrap();

    socket.send_to(b"Hello from the client!", destination).expect("Couldn't send data");

}
```

In this example, we create a UDP socket bound to the local address 127.0.0.1:8080 and send a datagram containing the message "Hello from the client!" to the address 127.0.0.1:8081.

Receiving Datagrams with recv_from()

To receive a datagram using a UDP socket, you use the recv_from() method. This method takes a mutable byte slice (&mut [u8]) as input and fills it with the received data. It also returns the number of bytes received and the address of the sender.

Rust

```rust
use std::net::UdpSocket;

fn main() {

    let socket = UdpSocket::bind("127.0.0.1:8080").unwrap();

    let mut buffer = [0; 1024];

    let (number_of_bytes, src_addr) = socket.recv_from(&mut buffer).expect("Didn't receive data");

    println!("Received {} bytes from {}: {:?}", number_of_bytes, src_addr, &buffer[..number_of_bytes]);

}
```

In this example, we create a UDP socket bound to the local address 127.0.0.1:8080 and wait for an incoming datagram. The recv_from() method fills the buffer with the received data and returns the number of bytes received and the sender's address.

Real-World Examples

UDP is often used in situations where speed and efficiency are more important than guaranteed delivery:

- Streaming media: Video and audio streaming services often use UDP because occasional packet loss is less noticeable than the delays that TCP might introduce.
- Online games: Many online games use UDP for real-time communication between players and the game server, as a slight delay or occasional packet loss is less critical than the overall responsiveness of the game.
- DNS: The Domain Name System (DNS) typically uses UDP for its queries and responses, as it prioritizes speed for quick name resolution.
- Time synchronization: The Network Time Protocol (NTP) uses UDP to synchronize clocks between computers.

Important Considerations

When working with UDP, keep these points in mind:

- Unreliability: UDP doesn't guarantee delivery or order of datagrams. If your application requires reliable communication, you'll need to implement your own mechanisms for handling packet loss and reordering.
- Packet Size: UDP datagrams have a limited size (typically around 65,507 bytes). If you need to send larger amounts of data, you'll need to split it into multiple datagrams.
- Congestion Control: UDP doesn't have built-in congestion control mechanisms like TCP. If your application sends a large amount of data, it might contribute to network congestion.

3.4 Socket Options and Configuration

You've learned the basics of creating and using sockets, but there's more to these powerful tools than meets the eye! Socket options allow you to fine-tune their behavior and customize them to suit your specific needs. Think of them as settings that you can adjust to optimize your network communication.

These options can affect various aspects of socket behavior, such as:

- Buffer sizes: You can control the size of the internal buffers used by the socket to store incoming and outgoing data.
- Timeouts: You can set timeouts for various socket operations, such as connecting to a server or receiving data.
- Reuse of addresses: You can allow the socket to bind to an address that is already in use, which can be useful in certain situations.
- Broadcast: You can enable or disable broadcast capabilities for UDP sockets.
- Multicast: You can configure multicast options for UDP sockets, allowing them to join multicast groups and receive data sent to those groups.

Setting Socket Options

Rust provides the set_nonblocking() and set_linger() methods on the TcpStream and UdpSocket types to configure socket options.

Here's an example of how you might set a socket option:

Rust

```rust
use std::net::{TcpStream, SocketAddr};

use std::time::Duration;

fn main() {

    let addr: SocketAddr = "127.0.0.1:8080".parse().unwrap();

    let stream = TcpStream::connect_timeout(&addr, Duration::from_secs(10)).unwrap();
```

```rust
    // ... use the stream ...
}
```

In this example, we set a connection timeout of 10 seconds on a TCP stream using the connect_timeout() method. This means that if the connection attempt takes longer than 10 seconds, it will fail with a timeout error.

Retrieving Socket Options

You can also retrieve the current value of a socket option using the get_linger() method.

Rust

```rust
use std::net::TcpStream;

fn main() {
    let stream = TcpStream::connect("127.0.0.1:8080").unwrap();

    match stream.linger() {
        Ok(linger) => {
            if let Some(duration) = linger {
                println!("Linger duration: {:?}", duration);
            } else {
                println!("Linger is disabled");
            }
        }
```

```
        Err(e) => {
            println!("Error getting linger option: {}", e);
        }
    }
}
```

In this example, we retrieve the linger option of a TCP stream using the linger() method. The linger option controls how long the operating system will keep trying to send data after the socket has been closed.

Platform-Specific Options

Keep in mind that some socket options are platform-specific. This means that they might not be available on all operating systems, or they might have different behaviors on different platforms. Refer to your operating system's documentation for details on the available socket options and their specific behaviors.

Real-World Examples

Socket options are used in various ways to optimize network applications:

- Tuning buffer sizes: Web servers might adjust buffer sizes to optimize for handling large files or many concurrent connections.
- Setting timeouts: Network clients might set timeouts to prevent indefinite waiting for responses from servers.
- Reusing addresses: Server applications might allow reuse of addresses to enable quick restarts after a crash.
- Configuring multicast: Applications that participate in multicast communication, such as video streaming or online

gaming, might need to configure multicast options on their sockets.

By understanding and utilizing socket options, you can gain finer control over your network communication and optimize your applications for specific needs and environments. As you gain more experience with network programming, you'll discover how these options can be powerful tools for fine-tuning your applications' performance and reliability.

Chapter 4: Asynchronous Programming with Tokio

Asynchronous programming is a powerful paradigm that allows your code to perform multiple tasks seemingly at the same time, without the overhead of traditional threads. It's like having a team of efficient chefs in a kitchen, each handling different parts of a meal preparation simultaneously, rather than having one chef do everything sequentially.

Tokio is a popular and robust asynchronous runtime for Rust. It provides the foundation for building high-performance network applications that can handle thousands of concurrent connections with ease.

4.1 Introduction to Asynchronous Programming

Let's explore the fascinating world of asynchronous programming! This powerful paradigm shifts the way we think about program execution, allowing us to write highly efficient and responsive network applications.

In the traditional synchronous programming model, operations happen one after another. When your code performs a task, such as reading from a file or waiting for a network request, it patiently waits until that task is complete before moving on to the next one. It's like following a recipe step-by-step – you can't start baking the cake until you've mixed all the ingredients.

Asynchronous programming, on the other hand, allows your code to initiate a task and then move on to other tasks without waiting for the first one to finish. It's like putting a kettle on to boil and then preparing your teacups and saucers while you wait for the water to heat up. Once the kettle whistles, you can pour the water and finish making your tea.

This "non-blocking" approach is particularly beneficial in network programming, where operations like waiting for data from a socket can take a significant amount of time. Instead of idly waiting, your program can utilize that time to perform other tasks, such as handling other client connections or performing background computations.

Benefits of Asynchronous Programming

Asynchronous programming offers several advantages, especially in the context of network applications:

- Increased Efficiency: By avoiding unnecessary waiting, your program can make better use of resources, such as CPU time and memory. This leads to improved performance and reduced resource consumption.
- Enhanced Responsiveness: Asynchronous applications can remain responsive to user input and other events even while performing long-running operations. This is crucial for providing a smooth and interactive user experience.
- Scalability: Asynchronous programming allows you to handle a large number of concurrent connections without the overhead of creating a separate thread for each connection. This makes it easier to build scalable network applications that can handle heavy loads.

How Asynchronous Programming Works

The key to asynchronous programming lies in the ability to perform operations without blocking the main thread of execution. This is typically achieved through mechanisms like callbacks, promises, or async/await (which we'll explore later in this chapter).

When an asynchronous operation is initiated, the program continues to execute other code while the operation is performed in the background. Once the operation is complete, the program is notified, and it can then process the result of the operation.

Real-World Examples

Asynchronous programming is used extensively in various domains:

- Web servers: Modern web servers like Nginx and Node.js rely heavily on asynchronous programming to handle thousands of concurrent connections efficiently.
- Mobile applications: Mobile apps often use asynchronous operations to perform tasks like downloading data or interacting with sensors without freezing the user interface.
- Real-time applications: Applications that require real-time responsiveness, such as online games and chat applications, often employ asynchronous techniques to handle network events and user interactions.
- Internet of Things (IoT): IoT devices often use asynchronous communication to handle sensor data and interact with cloud services.

The Event Loop

Many asynchronous runtimes, including Tokio, utilize an event loop to manage asynchronous operations. The event loop is like a central coordinator that continuously monitors for events, such as completed network requests or timer expirations. When an event occurs, the event loop dispatches the associated task to be processed.

This event-driven approach allows the program to efficiently handle multiple concurrent operations without the overhead of traditional threads.

4.2 The Tokio Runtime

In the context of asynchronous programming, a runtime is a special environment that provides the necessary infrastructure for executing asynchronous code. It handles tasks like scheduling tasks, managing threads, and providing an event loop to monitor for events like completed network requests or timer expirations.

The Tokio runtime is specifically designed for network programming and offers features that are crucial for building high-performance and scalable network applications.

Key Components of the Tokio Runtime

The Tokio runtime consists of several key components that work together to enable efficient asynchronous execution:

- Scheduler: The scheduler is responsible for managing and scheduling tasks. It determines which task should be executed next based on factors like priority and readiness.
- Executor: The executor is responsible for running tasks on threads. Tokio provides different types of executors, such as thread pool executors and single-threaded executors, to suit different needs.
- Event Loop: The event loop continuously monitors for events, such as completed network requests or timer expirations. When an event occurs, the event loop wakes up the corresponding task and allows it to continue its execution.
- I/O Driver: The I/O driver handles input/output operations, such as reading from and writing to sockets. It interacts with the operating system's I/O subsystem to perform these operations efficiently.
- Timer: The timer allows you to schedule tasks to be executed at specific times or after certain durations.

Using the Tokio Runtime

To use the Tokio runtime, you typically need to add the tokio crate to your project's dependencies and use the #[tokio::main] attribute on your main function.

Rust

```
use tokio::net::TcpListener;

#[tokio::main]

async fn main() {

    // Your asynchronous code here

}
```

This attribute sets up the Tokio runtime and enables the use of async/await syntax in your code. The runtime will automatically manage the execution of your asynchronous tasks.

Customizing the Runtime

Tokio provides options for customizing the runtime's behavior to suit your application's specific needs. You can configure things like the number of threads in the thread pool, the type of executor used, and various other parameters.

For example, you can create a runtime with a specific number of threads:

Rust

```
use tokio::runtime::Runtime;

fn main() {
```

```
    let rt = Runtime::new().unwrap();

    rt.block_on(async {

        // Your asynchronous code here

    });

}
```

This code creates a new runtime with the default configuration and then uses the block_on() method to run an asynchronous task on the runtime.

Real-World Examples

The Tokio runtime is used extensively in various high-performance network applications:

- Web servers: Hyper, a popular HTTP library for Rust, uses Tokio to build high-performance web servers that can handle thousands of concurrent connections.
- Messaging systems: Messaging platforms like Discord use Tokio to handle real-time communication between millions of users.
- Networking libraries: Many networking libraries in the Rust ecosystem, such as request (an HTTP client) and tokio-postgres (a PostgreSQL database driver), are built on top of Tokio.

Benefits of Using Tokio

Tokio offers several benefits for building asynchronous applications:

- Performance: Tokio is highly optimized for performance and can handle a large number of concurrent connections with minimal overhead.

- Scalability: Tokio's architecture allows you to build scalable applications that can handle increasing loads without sacrificing performance.
- Ease of Use: Tokio provides a user-friendly API and abstractions that make it easier to write asynchronous code.
- Ecosystem: Tokio has a large and growing ecosystem of libraries and tools that can help you build various network applications.

Understanding the Tokio runtime and its capabilities, you gain a powerful tool for building high-performance and scalable network applications in Rust. It's your gateway to the world of asynchronous programming, enabling you to write efficient and responsive code that can handle the demands of modern network environments.

4.3 Futures, Tasks, and Executors

Alright, let's break down the core concepts that make asynchronous programming in Rust tick: Futures, Tasks, and Executors. These are the building blocks that enable you to write efficient and concurrent code that can handle many operations seemingly at the same time.

Futures

Imagine you order a pizza. You don't get the pizza immediately; instead, you get a promise that the pizza will be ready in some time. A Future in Rust is similar to this promise. It represents a value that might not be available yet but will be eventually.

More formally, a Future is an asynchronous computation that produces a value at some point in the future. This value could be anything: a network response, the result of a file read, or a computed value. The key is that the value isn't available immediately; it needs some time to be computed.

In Rust, Futures are represented by the Future trait. This trait defines a poll() method that can be called to check if the future has completed. If the future is ready, poll() returns the computed value. Otherwise, it indicates that the future is still pending.

Rust

```
trait Future {

    type Output;

    fn poll(self: Pin<&mut Self>, cx: &mut Context<'_>) -> Poll<Self::Output>;

}
```

Don't worry too much about the details of the poll() method for now. We'll explore how to work with futures using async/await syntax later in this chapter, which provides a more ergonomic way to handle asynchronous operations.

Tasks

A Task is an asynchronous operation that is being executed by the Tokio runtime. Think of it as a unit of work that the runtime manages and schedules. Each task represents an independent asynchronous computation that can make progress concurrently with other tasks.

When you spawn a future using tokio::spawn(), the runtime creates a new task to execute that future. The runtime then manages the execution of this task, ensuring that it makes progress without blocking other tasks.

Executors

Executors are the workhorses of the Tokio runtime. They are responsible for running tasks on threads. Tokio provides different types of executors to suit different needs:

- **Thread Pool Executor:** This executor uses a pool of threads to execute tasks concurrently. It's a good choice for applications that need to handle many concurrent operations.
- **Single-Threaded Executor:** This executor runs all tasks on a single thread. It's suitable for applications that don't require high concurrency or have specific threading requirements.

The executor manages the scheduling and execution of tasks, ensuring that they make progress efficiently. It interacts with the operating system's scheduler to distribute tasks across threads and utilizes an event loop to monitor for events and wake up tasks that are ready to continue.

Futures, tasks, and executors work together seamlessly in the Tokio runtime to enable efficient asynchronous execution:

1. You create a future that represents an asynchronous operation.
2. You spawn the future using tokio::spawn(), which creates a new task.
3. The executor manages the execution of the task, scheduling it on a thread and polling its future to check for completion.
4. When the future is ready, the executor retrieves the computed value and makes it available to the rest of your code.

Real-World Examples

Futures, tasks, and executors are the foundation of many asynchronous applications:

- Web servers: Web servers use futures to represent incoming requests and tasks to handle those requests concurrently. Executors ensure that these tasks are executed efficiently on available threads.
- Database drivers: Asynchronous database drivers use futures to represent database queries and tasks to manage the execution of those queries.
- Real-time applications: Real-time applications use futures and tasks to handle network events and user interactions in a non-blocking manner.

Understanding these core concepts, you gain a deeper understanding of how asynchronous programming works in Rust. This knowledge will be invaluable as you start building more complex and sophisticated asynchronous applications using Tokio.

4.4 Asynchronous TCP and UDP Sockets

Alright, now let's bring together our knowledge of asynchronous programming and sockets! Tokio provides asynchronous versions of the TCP and UDP sockets we explored in Chapter 3. These asynchronous sockets allow you to perform network operations without blocking the execution of other tasks, making your applications more efficient and responsive.

Asynchronous TCP Sockets

Remember how we used std::net::TcpListener and std::net::TcpStream for synchronous TCP communication? Well, Tokio offers their asynchronous counterparts: tokio::net::TcpListener and tokio::net::TcpStream.

These asynchronous versions work similarly to their synchronous counterparts, but they operate in a non-blocking manner. This means that operations like accepting connections or reading and writing data don't block the execution of other tasks. Instead, they return futures that resolve when the operation is complete.

Here's an example of how you might use tokio::net::TcpListener to create an asynchronous TCP server:

Rust

```
use tokio::net::TcpListener;

#[tokio::main]

async fn main() {

    let listener = TcpListener::bind("127.0.0.1:8080").await.unwrap();

    println!("Server listening on port 8080");

    loop {

        let (mut socket, _) = listener.accept().await.unwrap();

        tokio::spawn(async move {

            // Process the connection asynchronously

            let mut buffer = [0; 1024];

            loop {

                match socket.read(&mut buffer).await {

                    Ok(0) => break, // Connection closed
```

```
                    Ok(n) => {
                        if socket.write_all(&buffer[..n]).await.is_err() {
                            break; // Error writing to socket
                        }
                    }
                    Err(e) => {
                        println!("Error: {}", e);
                        break;
                    }
                }
            }
        });
    }
}
```

In this example:

- We create an asynchronous TCP listener using TcpListener::bind().
- We use a loop to continuously accept incoming connections.
- For each connection, we spawn a new asynchronous task using tokio::spawn().
- Within the task, we handle the client communication asynchronously using socket.read() and socket.write_all().

Asynchronous UDP Sockets

Similarly, Tokio provides tokio::net::UdpSocket for asynchronous UDP communication. You can use this type to send and receive datagrams without blocking the execution of other tasks.

Rust

```
use tokio::net::UdpSocket;

#[tokio::main]

async fn main() {

    let socket =
UdpSocket::bind("127.0.0.1:8080").await.unwrap();

    println!("UDP socket bound to port 8080");

    let mut buffer = [0; 1024];

    loop {

        let (number_of_bytes, src_addr) =
socket.recv_from(&mut
buffer).await.expect("Didn't receive data");

        println!("Received {} bytes from {}: {:?}", number_of_bytes, src_addr,
&buffer[..number_of_bytes]);

        // Echo the data back to the sender
        let _ =
socket.send_to(&buffer[..number_of_bytes],
&src_addr).await;

    }

}
```

In this example:

- We create an asynchronous UDP socket using UdpSocket::bind().
- We use a loop to continuously receive datagrams.
- For each received datagram, we print the data and echo it back to the sender.

Benefits of Asynchronous Sockets

Asynchronous sockets offer several benefits for network programming:

- Efficiency: They allow you to handle multiple connections concurrently without the overhead of creating a separate thread for each connection.
- Responsiveness: They prevent your application from blocking while waiting for network operations, keeping it responsive to user input and other events.
- Scalability: They make it easier to build scalable network applications that can handle a large number of concurrent connections.

Real-World Examples

Asynchronous sockets are used extensively in high-performance network applications:

- Web servers: Asynchronous web servers use asynchronous TCP sockets to handle thousands of concurrent client connections.
- Chat applications: Asynchronous chat applications use asynchronous sockets to handle real-time message exchange between users.
- Game servers: Asynchronous game servers use asynchronous sockets to handle communication between players and the game server.

4.5 Handling Multiple Connections Concurrently

Handling multiple connections concurrently is essential for building responsive and scalable network applications that can efficiently serve many clients simultaneously.

Think of a busy restaurant: a single waiter can only handle a limited number of tables at a time. To serve more customers efficiently, the restaurant needs multiple waiters working concurrently. Similarly, a network server needs to handle multiple client connections concurrently to provide a smooth and responsive experience for all users.

Why Concurrency Matters

In network programming, concurrency is essential for several reasons:

- Responsiveness: If your server handles each client connection sequentially, it can become unresponsive to other clients while processing a long-running request. Concurrency allows the server to handle multiple clients simultaneously, ensuring that each client receives timely responses.
- Efficiency: Concurrency allows your server to utilize system resources more effectively. Instead of waiting idly for one client to finish, the server can process requests from other clients, maximizing CPU utilization and throughput.
- Scalability: Concurrency is crucial for building scalable network applications. As the number of clients increases, a concurrent server can handle the growing load by distributing the work across multiple tasks or threads.

Concurrency with Tokio

Tokio provides powerful tools for handling multiple connections concurrently. The key is to use tokio::spawn() to create a separate asynchronous task for each client connection. This allows each connection to be processed independently without blocking the main thread or other connections.

Here's an example of an asynchronous TCP server that handles multiple connections concurrently:

Rust

```
use tokio::net::TcpListener;

#[tokio::main]

async fn main() {

    let listener = TcpListener::bind("127.0.0.1:8080").await.unwrap();

    println!("Server listening on port 8080");[1]

    loop {

        let (mut socket, _) = listener.accept().await.unwrap();

        tokio::spawn(async move {

            // Process the connection asynchronously

            let mut buffer = [0; 1024];

            loop {
```

```
            match socket.read(&mut buffer).await {
                Ok(0) => break, // Connection closed
                Ok(n) => {
                    if socket.write_all(&buffer[..n]).await.is_err() {
                        break; // Error writing to socket
                    }
                }
                Err(e) => {
                    println!("Error: {}", e);
                    break;
                }
            }
        });
    }
}
```

In this example, for each incoming connection, we create a new asynchronous task using tokio::spawn(). This task handles the client communication independently, allowing the server to accept and process other connections concurrently.

Sharing Data and Synchronization

When handling multiple connections concurrently, you might need to share data between tasks or synchronize their access to shared resources. Tokio provides tools like channels and mutexes to help you manage shared data safely and efficiently.

We'll explore these concurrency primitives in more detail in later chapters.

Real-World Examples

Handling multiple connections concurrently is a fundamental requirement for many network applications:

- Web servers: Web servers handle thousands of concurrent connections from users browsing the web.
- Chat applications: Chat servers handle multiple users exchanging messages in real time.
- Game servers: Game servers handle multiple players interacting in a shared game environment.
- Streaming services: Streaming services handle multiple users streaming video or audio content concurrently.

By utilizing Tokio's concurrency features, you can build network applications that are responsive, efficient, and scalable, capable of handling the demands of modern network environments.

Chapter 5: Serialization and Deserialization

Alright, let's talk about how to transform data into a format suitable for sending over a network or storing in a file. This process is called **serialization**. Think of it like packing a suitcase for a trip – you need to organize your belongings neatly so they fit compactly and can be easily unpacked at your destination.

Similarly, when you send data over a network, you need to convert it into a format that can be transmitted efficiently and reliably. This might involve converting complex data structures, like structs and enums, into a stream of bytes. The reverse process, converting a stream of bytes back into usable data structures, is called **deserialization**. It's like unpacking your suitcase at your destination and putting everything back in its place.

In this chapter, we'll explore different serialization formats, including JSON, XML, and Protobuf, and learn how to use them in Rust with the help of the `serde` framework. We'll also see how to implement custom serialization for your own data types.

5.1 JSON with serde_json

JSON (JavaScript Object Notation) is a popular and human-readable data format that's widely used for web APIs and data exchange. It's like a universal language that many different systems and programming languages can understand.

Rust provides excellent support for JSON serialization and deserialization through the `serde_json` crate. This crate is built on top of the `serde` framework, which provides a powerful and flexible way to work with various serialization formats.

Serializing Data to JSON

Let's explore how to serialize data into JSON format in Rust. Remember that serialization is like carefully packing your belongings into a suitcase for a trip. In this case, we're transforming Rust data structures into a neat and compact JSON representation that can be easily sent over a network or stored in a file.

JSON (JavaScript Object Notation) is a popular and versatile data format that's widely used for data exchange on the web and beyond. It's known for its human-readable syntax and its compatibility with various programming languages.

The serde_json Crate

Rust provides excellent support for JSON serialization through the serde_json crate. This crate is built on top of the serde framework, which provides a powerful and flexible way to work with various serialization formats.

To use serde_json, you'll need to add it as a dependency in your Cargo.toml file:

Ini, TOML

```ini
[dependencies]

serde_json = "1.0" // Replace with the desired version

serde = { version = "1.0", features = ["derive"] } // Replace with the desired version
```

The Serialize Trait

To serialize a data structure into JSON, it needs to implement the Serialize trait from the serde crate. This trait tells serde how to convert the data structure into its JSON representation.

The easiest way to implement the Serialize trait is to use the #[derive(Serialize)] attribute on your struct or enum. This automatically generates the necessary code for serialization.

```rust
use serde::Serialize;

#[derive(Serialize)]
struct User {
    name: String,
    age: u32,
}
```

In this example, we define a User struct and mark it as Serialize using the #[derive(Serialize)] attribute. This tells serde that we want to be able to serialize this struct into JSON.

Serializing with to_string()

Once your data structure implements the Serialize trait, you can serialize it to JSON using the serde_json::to_string() function. This function takes a reference to the value you want to serialize and returns a Result containing the JSON string representation.

```rust
use serde_json;

fn main() {
```

```rust
    let user = User {
        name: String::from("Alice"),
        age: 30,
    };
    let json_string = serde_json::to_string(&user).unwrap();
    println!("Serialized user: {}", json_string);
    // Output: {"name":"Alice","age":30}
}
```

In this example, we create a User object and serialize it to a JSON string using serde_json::to_string(). The unwrap() method is used to handle potential errors during the serialization process.

Handling Serialization Errors

The to_string() function returns a Result because the serialization process might encounter errors. For example, if your data structure contains a value that cannot be represented in JSON (like a raw pointer), the serialization will fail.

It's important to handle these potential errors gracefully in your code. You can use techniques like match expressions or the ? operator to handle errors and prevent your program from crashing.

Real-World Examples

Serializing data to JSON is a common task in many network applications:

- Web APIs: When building web APIs, you often need to serialize data into JSON format to send it to clients as a response.
- Configuration files: You can use JSON to store configuration settings for your application, making it easy to read and modify these settings.
- Data exchange: JSON is often used to exchange data between different systems or applications, as it's a widely supported and understood format.

While to_string() is a convenient way to serialize data to a JSON string, serde_json provides other functions for serializing data to different destinations, such as files or network streams.

For example, you can use serde_json::to_writer() to serialize data to a file:

Rust

```rust
use std::fs::File;

use serde_json;

fn main() {
    let user = User {

        name: String::from("Alice"),

        age: 30,

    };

    let file = File::create("user.json").unwrap();

    serde_json::to_writer_pretty(file, &user).unwrap();
```

}

This code snippet serializes the User object to a file named "user.json" with pretty formatting.

By mastering the techniques of JSON serialization with serde_json, you gain a valuable tool for handling data in your network applications. You can efficiently transform your Rust data structures into a portable and widely understood format, ready to be exchanged with other systems or stored for later use.

Deserializing JSON Data

Alright, now that we've packed our data neatly into a JSON suitcase, let's learn how to unpack it at the other end! Deserialization is the process of converting a JSON string back into usable Rust data structures. It's like arriving at your destination, opening your suitcase, and putting everything back in its rightful place.

The Deserialize Trait

Just as we used the Serialize trait to serialize data, we'll use the Deserialize trait from the serde crate to deserialize JSON data. This trait tells serde how to convert a JSON string into the corresponding Rust data structure.

Similar to serialization, the easiest way to implement the Deserialize trait is to use the #[derive(Deserialize)] attribute on your struct or enum.

Rust

```
use serde::Deserialize;

#[derive(Deserialize)]
```

```rust
struct User {
    name: String,
    age: u32,
}
```

This code snippet defines a User struct and derives the Deserialize trait for it. Now, serde knows how to convert a JSON string representing a user into a User object.

Deserializing with from_str()

To deserialize a JSON string, you use the serde_json::from_str() function. This function takes the JSON string as input and returns a Result containing the deserialized value.

Rust

```rust
use serde_json;

fn main() {
    let json_string = r#"{"name":"Alice","age":30}"#;

    let user: User = serde_json::from_str(json_string).unwrap();

    println!("Deserialized user: {:?}", user); // Output: User { name: "Alice", age: 30 }
}
```

In this example, we deserialize the JSON string r#"{"name":"Alice","age":30}"# into a User object using serde_json::from_str(). The unwrap() method is used to handle potential errors during the deserialization process.

100

Handling Deserialization Errors

The from_str() function returns a Result because the deserialization process might encounter errors. This can happen if the JSON string is malformed, if it doesn't match the expected structure of your Rust data type, or if it contains values that cannot be converted to the corresponding Rust types.

It's crucial to handle these potential errors gracefully in your code. You can use techniques like match expressions or the ? operator to handle errors and prevent your program from crashing.

Real-World Examples

Deserializing JSON data is a common task in many network applications:

- Web APIs: When receiving data from a web API, you often need to deserialize the JSON response into Rust data structures to process it.
- Configuration files: You can use JSON to store configuration settings for your application. Deserializing the JSON file allows you to load these settings into your program.
- Data exchange: When receiving data from other systems or applications in JSON format, deserialization allows you to convert it into a usable form in your Rust program.

While from_str() is a convenient way to deserialize a JSON string, serde_json provides other functions for deserializing data from different sources, such as files or network streams.

For example, you can use serde_json::from_reader() to deserialize data from a file:

Rust

```rust
use std::fs::File;

use serde_json;

fn main() {

    let file = File::open("user.json").unwrap();

    let user: User = serde_json::from_reader(file).unwrap();

    println!("Deserialized user: {:?}", user);

}
```

This code snippet deserializes a User object from a file named "user.json".

By mastering the techniques of JSON deserialization with serde_json, you gain the ability to effectively handle incoming JSON data in your network applications. You can seamlessly convert JSON data into your Rust data structures, making it readily available for processing and use within your program.

Working with JSON in Network Applications

Let's bring together our knowledge of JSON serialization and deserialization and see how it plays a crucial role in network applications! JSON's human-readable format and broad compatibility make it a popular choice for exchanging data between clients and servers.

Think of JSON as a universal language that both your Rust application and the remote server can understand. By serializing your data into JSON before sending it over the network, you ensure that the server can correctly interpret and process it. Similarly, when receiving data from the server, deserializing the

JSON response allows you to easily work with the data in your Rust application.

Sending JSON Data

When sending data to a server, you typically need to serialize it into JSON format first. This ensures that the data is transmitted in a format that the server can understand.

Here's an example of how you might send a JSON message over a TCP connection:

```Rust
use serde::{Serialize, Deserialize};

use serde_json;

use tokio::net::TcpStream;

use tokio::io::{AsyncReadExt, AsyncWriteExt};

#[derive(Serialize, Deserialize)]

struct Request {

    method: String,

    data: String,

}

#[tokio::main]

async fn main() {
```

```rust
    let mut stream = TcpStream::connect("127.0.0.1:8080").await.unwrap();

    let request = Request {
        method: String::from("getData"),
        data: String::from("some data"),
    };

    let json_string = serde_json::to_string(&request).unwrap();

stream.write_all(json_string.as_bytes()).await.unwrap();

    // ... receive a response from the server ...
}
```

In this example, we define a `Request` struct and serialize it into a JSON string using `serde_json::to_string()`. We then send this JSON string over the TCP stream using `stream.write_all()`.

Receiving JSON Data

When receiving data from a server, you'll often receive it in JSON format. You then need to deserialize this JSON data into your Rust data structures to process it.

Here's an example of how you might receive and deserialize a JSON response from a server:

Rust

```rust
// ... (previous code) ...
```

```
let mut buffer = [0; 1024];

let bytes_read = stream.read(&mut
buffer).await.unwrap();

let response: Response =
serde_json::from_slice(&buffer[..bytes_read]).unw
rap();

// ... process the response ...
```

In this example, we receive data from the TCP stream into a buffer and then deserialize it into a Response struct using serde_json::from_slice().

Real-World Examples

Working with JSON in network applications is extremely common:

- Web APIs: Web APIs often use JSON as the primary data format for requests and responses. Clients serialize their requests into JSON, and servers respond with JSON data.
- Microservices: Microservices architectures often use JSON for communication between different services.
- Data streaming: JSON can be used to stream data between applications, such as sending real-time updates or log messages.
- Configuration management: Configuration management tools often use JSON to store and exchange configuration data.

Best Practices

When working with JSON in network applications, keep these best practices in mind:

- Error Handling: Always handle potential errors during serialization and deserialization. Network communication

can be unreliable, and JSON data might not always be in the expected format.
- Data Validation: Validate the received JSON data to ensure that it conforms to your expectations. This helps prevent unexpected errors or security vulnerabilities.
- Efficiency: Consider the size of your JSON data, especially if you're dealing with large datasets or frequent communication. You might want to use techniques like compression or more efficient serialization formats like Protobuf for performance-critical applications.

Understanding how to work with JSON in network applications, you gain a valuable skill for building robust and interoperable systems. JSON's popularity and versatility make it a great choice for exchanging data in various network environments.

5.2 Other Serialization Formats

While JSON is a popular and versatile choice for data serialization, it's not the only option available. Different serialization formats have different strengths and weaknesses, making them suitable for various use cases. Let's explore two other prominent formats: XML and Protobuf.

XML (Extensible Markup Language)

XML is a markup language that defines a set of rules for encoding documents in a format that is both human-readable and machine-readable. It uses tags to structure data and define elements and attributes.

Think of XML as a way to represent data in a hierarchical structure, similar to how HTML is used to structure web pages. XML is often used for more complex data structures and in situations where strict validation and schema enforcement are required.

Working with XML in Rust

Rust provides several crates for working with XML, including serde_xml_rs and quick-xml. These crates offer different approaches to parsing and generating XML data.

Here's a simple example using serde_xml_rs to serialize a Rust struct to XML:

```Rust
use serde::Serialize;

use serde_xml_rs::to_string;

#[derive(Serialize)]
struct User {
    name: String,
    age: u32,
}
fn main() {
    let user = User {
        name: String::from("Alice"),
        age: 30,
    };

    let xml_string = to_string(&user).unwrap();
```

```
    println!("Serialized user: {}", xml_string);

    // Output:
<User><name>Alice</name><age>30</age></User>

}
```

In this example, we define a User struct and serialize it to XML using serde_xml_rs::to_string().

Real-World Examples of XML

XML is often used in enterprise applications, web services, and data exchange formats:

- SOAP (Simple Object Access Protocol): SOAP is a messaging protocol that uses XML to exchange structured information in web services.
- RSS (Really Simple Syndication): RSS is a web feed format that uses XML to publish frequently updated content, such as blog posts and news headlines.
- Microsoft Office documents: Microsoft Office documents like Word (.docx) and Excel (.xlsx) are based on XML formats.
- Configuration files: Many applications use XML for configuration files due to its structured format and human readability.

Protobuf (Protocol Buffers)

Protobuf is a binary serialization format developed by Google. It's designed to be efficient, compact, and fast to parse, making it well-suited for network communication and data storage.

Think of Protobuf as a more streamlined and optimized way to serialize data compared to JSON or XML. It uses a binary encoding that reduces the size of the serialized data, which can be beneficial for bandwidth-constrained environments or when dealing with large datasets.

Working with Protobuf in Rust

Rust provides crates like prost and protobuf for working with Protobuf. These crates allow you to define message formats using Protobuf's language and then generate Rust code to serialize and deserialize those messages.

Here's a basic example using prost to define a Protobuf message and serialize it:

Rust

```rust
use prost::Message;

#[derive(Clone, PartialEq, Message)]
struct User {
    #[prost(string, tag="1")]
    name: String,
    #[prost(int32, tag="2")]
    age: i32,
}

fn main() {
    let user = User {
        name: String::from("Alice"),
        age: 30,
```

```
    };

    let mut buffer = Vec::new();

    user.encode(&mut buffer).unwrap();

    println!("Serialized user (bytes): {:?}",
buffer);

}
```

In this example, we define a User message using Protobuf's syntax and then serialize it into a byte buffer using prost::Message::encode().

Real-World Examples of Protobuf

Protobuf is used in various applications where performance and efficiency are critical:

- gRPC: gRPC is a high-performance remote procedure call framework that uses Protobuf as its default serialization format.
- Data storage: Protobuf is often used for storing data in files or databases due to its compact size and efficient parsing.
- Network communication: Many network applications use Protobuf for communication between clients and servers, especially when dealing with large amounts of data or bandwidth-constrained environments.

Choosing the Right Format

The choice of serialization format depends on several factors:

- Human readability: JSON and XML are human-readable, while Protobuf is binary.
- Performance: Protobuf is generally more efficient and compact than JSON or XML.

- Compatibility: JSON is widely supported across different programming languages and systems.
- Schema enforcement: XML supports schema validation, which can be useful for ensuring data integrity.
- Specific requirements: Some applications might have specific requirements that dictate the use of a particular format.

Understanding the strengths and weaknesses of different serialization formats, you can choose the most appropriate one for your network application.

5.3 Custom Serialization

You've seen how `serde` makes it easy to serialize and deserialize data using common formats like JSON, XML, and Protobuf. But what if you need to handle a unique data format or have specific requirements for how your data is represented? That's where custom serialization comes in!

Custom serialization allows you to take full control of the serialization and deserialization process. You can define precisely how your data is transformed into a byte stream or any other representation. This can be particularly useful when:

- Dealing with proprietary formats: You might need to interact with a system that uses a custom data format not supported by standard libraries.
- Optimizing for performance: You might need to optimize the serialization process for specific performance requirements, such as minimizing data size or maximizing throughput.
- Implementing special logic: You might need to implement special handling for certain data types or values, such as encrypting sensitive data or encoding data in a specific way.

The serde Traits

serde provides a set of traits that allow you to implement custom serialization and deserialization. The key traits are:

- **Serializer**: This trait defines methods for serializing data into various output formats. You implement this trait for your custom serializer to define how data should be converted into the desired format.
- **Deserializer**: This trait defines methods for deserializing data from various input formats. You implement this trait for your custom deserializer to define how data should be parsed and converted back into Rust data structures.

Example

Let's illustrate custom serialization with a simple example. Suppose you have a Point struct that represents a point in 2D space:

```Rust
struct Point {
    x: i32,
    y: i32,
}
```

You want to serialize this struct into a custom format where the coordinates are represented as a comma-separated string, like this: "x,y".

Here's how you might implement a custom serializer for this format:

```Rust
use serde::{Serialize, Serializer};

struct Point {
    x: i32,
    y: i32,
}

impl Serialize for Point {
    fn serialize<S>(&self, serializer: S) -> Result<S::Ok, S::Error>
    where
        S: Serializer,
    {
        let s = format!("{},{}", self.x, self.y);
        serializer.serialize_str(&s)
    }
}

fn main() {
    let point = Point { x: 10, y: 20 };
    let serialized = serde_json::to_string(&point).unwrap();
```

```
    println!("Serialized point: {}", serialized);
// Output: "10,20"

}
```

In this example, we implement the Serialize trait for the Point struct. In the serialize() method, we format the coordinates into a comma-separated string and then use the serializer.serialize_str() method to serialize it as a string.

Implementing a Deserializer

To deserialize data from our custom format, you would implement the Deserializer trait. This would involve parsing the comma-separated string and extracting the x and y coordinates.

Real-World Examples

Custom serialization can be useful in various situations:

- Game development: Game developers often use custom serialization formats to store game data efficiently or to handle specific data structures used in their games.
- Embedded systems: Embedded systems might use custom serialization formats to optimize for limited memory or bandwidth.
- Financial applications: Financial applications might use custom serialization formats to ensure data security or comply with specific regulations.

Advanced Techniques

serde provides advanced techniques for handling more complex serialization scenarios, such as:

- Visitor pattern: The visitor pattern allows you to define custom serialization logic for different data types.

- Zero-copy serialization: Zero-copy serialization avoids unnecessary data copying, which can improve performance.
- Serialization with lifetime parameters: You can implement serialization for types with lifetime parameters, which can be useful for handling borrowed data.

By mastering custom serialization with `serde`, you gain a powerful tool for handling data transformation in your network applications. You can define precisely how your data is serialized and deserialized, giving you full control over the process and enabling you to meet specific requirements and optimize for performance.

Chapter 6: Building a Robust Web Server

In this chapter, we'll learn how to build a robust web server in Rust using the hyper crate. We'll explore the HTTP protocol and the request/response cycle, learn how to handle different routes and requests, serve static files, and even use templates to generate dynamic content.

6.1 HTTP and Request/Response Cycle

Before we fire up our code editor and start churning out Rust code, let's take a step back and understand the fundamental protocol that makes the web tick: HTTP (Hypertext Transfer Protocol). Think of HTTP as the language that web browsers and web servers use to communicate with each other. It's a set of rules that govern how clients request resources from servers and how servers respond to those requests.

The Request/Response Cycle

At the heart of HTTP is the request/response cycle. It's like a conversation between a client (your web browser) and a server (the machine hosting the website you're trying to access). This conversation follows a clear pattern:

1. The client initiates a request: When you type a URL into your browser or click a link, your browser sends an HTTP request to the server hosting that website. This request is like a letter addressed to the server, containing information about what the client wants.
2. The server receives the request: The server, which is constantly listening for incoming requests, receives the client's request and examines it.

3. The server processes the request: Based on the information in the request, the server figures out what to do. This might involve fetching a web page from its storage, running a script to generate dynamic content, or accessing a database to retrieve information.
4. The server sends a response: Once the server has processed the request, it sends back an HTTP response to the client. This response is like a reply to the client's letter, containing the requested information or a message indicating whether the request was successful.
5. The client receives the response: Your browser receives the server's response and interprets it. If the response contains a web page, the browser renders it and displays it to you. If the response indicates an error, the browser might display an error message.

Components of an HTTP Request

An HTTP request contains several key pieces of information:

- **Method:** This indicates the type of action the client wants the server to perform. Common methods include:
    - GET: Retrieve a resource (like a web page or an image).
    - POST: Submit data to the server (like a form submission).
    - PUT: Update an existing resource.
    - DELETE: Delete a resource.
- **URL (Uniform Resource Locator):** This specifies the address of the resource the client is requesting. It includes the domain name (e.g., example.com), the path to the resource (e.g., /articles/123), and optionally, query parameters (e.g., ?search=rust).
- **Headers:** These provide additional information about the request, such as the client's preferred language, the type of content it can accept, and any cookies it wants to send.

- **Body:** This is optional and contains data that the client is sending to the server, such as form data or JSON payload.

Components of an HTTP Response

An HTTP response also contains key information:

- **Status code:** This indicates whether the request was successful. Common status codes include:
    - 200 OK: The request was successful.
    - 404 Not Found: The requested resource was not found.
    - 500 Internal Server Error:1 An error occurred on the server.2
- **Headers:** These provide additional information about the response, such as the content type (e.g., text/html, application/json), the length of the content, and any cookies the server wants to set.
- **Body:** This contains the actual content of the response, such as the HTML of a web page, an image file, or a JSON data structure.

Real-World Examples

The HTTP request/response cycle is the foundation of how we interact with the web:

- Browsing a website: When you visit a website, your browser sends a GET request to the server, and the server responds with the HTML of the web page.
- Submitting a form: When you fill out a form and submit it, your browser sends a POST request to the server with the form data in the request body.
- Downloading a file: When you download a file, your browser sends a GET request, and the server responds with the file content in the response body.

- Accessing an API: When you use an application that interacts with a web API, the application sends HTTP requests to the API endpoints and receives JSON or XML data in the responses.

Understanding the HTTP request/response cycle is crucial for building web applications and services. It provides the framework for how clients and servers communicate and exchange information, enabling the rich and interactive experiences we enjoy on the web.

6.2 Building a Basic HTTP Server with hyper

Let's build a basic HTTP server in Rust using the hyper crate! hyper is a fast and robust HTTP library that provides the building blocks for creating web servers and clients. It's like having a set of powerful tools and machinery to construct your very own web server from the ground up.

Before we start, make sure you have hyper added as a dependency in your Cargo.toml file:

Ini, TOML

```
[dependencies]

hyper = "0.14" # Replace with the desired version

tokio = { version = "1.0", features = ["full"] }
# Replace with the desired version
```

Now, let's create a simple server that responds with "Hello, world!" to every request:

Rust

```
use hyper::{Body, Request, Response, Server};

use hyper::service::{make_service_fn, service_fn};

use std::convert::Infallible;

async fn¹ handle_request(_req: Request<Body>) -> Result<Response<Body>, Infallible>² {

    Ok(Response::new(Body::from("Hello, world!")))

}

#[tokio::main]

async fn main() {

    let addr³ = ([127, 0, 0, 1], 3000).into();

    let make_svc = make_service_fn(|_conn| async {

        Ok::<_, Infallible>(service_fn(handle_request))

    });

    let server = Server::bind(&addr).serve(make_svc);⁴

    println!("Server running on http://{}", addr);

    if let Err(e) = server.await {
```

```
        eprintln!("server⁵ error: {}", e);
    }
}
```

Let's break down this code snippet step-by-step:

1. Import necessary modules: We import the necessary modules from `hyper` for handling requests, responses, and the server itself.
2. Define the request handler: The `handle_request` function is where the magic happens. It takes a `Request<Body>` object as input, which represents the incoming HTTP request. In this basic example, we ignore the request details and simply return a `Response<Body>` with the text "Hello, world!" in the body. The `Infallible` type indicates that this function will never return an error.
3. Create a service: We use `make_service_fn` and `service_fn` to create a service that handles incoming requests. These functions are part of `hyper`'s service framework, which provides a way to abstract the handling of requests and responses.
4. Bind and serve: We bind the server to the address `127.0.0.1:3000` using `Server::bind(&addr)`. This tells the server to listen for incoming connections on that specific address. Then, we use `serve(make_svc)` to start the server and begin accepting requests.
5. Run the server: The `server.await` line starts the server and runs it until an error occurs or it's explicitly stopped.

Now, if you compile and run this code, you've just created your own web server! Open your web browser and visit http://127.0.0.1:3000. You should see the friendly greeting "Hello, world!" displayed on the page.

This is a very basic example, but it demonstrates the core principles of building an HTTP server with hyper. As we progress through this chapter, we'll explore more advanced techniques for handling different types of requests, routing, serving static files, and generating dynamic content.

6.3 Routing and Handling Requests

Let's add some intelligence to our web server! In the previous section, we created a basic server that responded with the same message to every request. But in a real-world application, you'll want to handle different requests differently, depending on the requested URL, the HTTP method, and other factors. This is where routing comes into play.

Think of routing as a traffic controller that directs incoming requests to the appropriate handlers based on certain rules. It's like having a receptionist who directs visitors to different departments based on their purpose of visit.

Routing with hyper

While hyper itself doesn't provide built-in routing functionalities, it can be easily combined with other crates to achieve flexible routing. One popular choice is the matchit crate, which provides efficient and flexible route matching.

First, add matchit to your Cargo.toml file:

```ini
Ini, TOML

[dependencies]

matchit = "0.5" # Replace with the desired version
```

Now, let's create a server that handles different routes:

```Rust
use hyper::{Body, Request, Response, Server};

use hyper::service::{make_service_fn, service_fn};

use std::convert::Infallible;

use matchit::Router;

async fn handle_request(req: Request<Body>) -> Result<Response<Body>, Infallible> {

    let mut router = Router::new();

    router.insert("/", || async {
Ok(Response::new(Body::from("Welcome to the homepage!"))) }).unwrap();

    router.insert("/hello/:name", |caps| async move {

        let name = &caps["name"];


Ok(Response::new(Body::from(format!("Hello, {}!", name))))

    }).unwrap();

    match router.at(req.uri().path()) {

        Ok(matched) => {


(matched.value)(&matched.params).await
```

```rust
        }
        Err(_) => {
            Ok(Response::builder()
                .status(404)
                .body(Body::from("Not Found"))
                .unwrap())
        }
    }
}

#[tokio::main]
async fn main() {
    let addr = ([127, 0, 0, 1], 3000).into();

    let make_svc = make_service_fn(|_conn| async {
        Ok::<_, Infallible>(service_fn(handle_request))
    });

    let server = Server::bind(&addr).serve(make_svc);[1]

    println!("Server running on http://{}", addr);

    if let Err(e) = server.await {
```

```
        eprintln!("server error: {}", e);
    }
}
```

In this example:

- We[2] create a Router from the matchit crate.
- We define two routes:
    - /: This route matches the root path and responds with "Welcome to the homepage!".
    - /hello/:name: This route matches paths like /hello/Alice or /hello/Bob and extracts the name parameter from the URL.
- We use router.at(req.uri().path()) to match the incoming request's path against the defined routes.
- If a route matches, we execute the corresponding handler.
- If no route matches, we return a 404 Not Found response.

Handling Different HTTP Methods

You can also handle different HTTP methods (GET, POST, PUT, DELETE, etc.) for the same route. This allows you to define different behavior for different types of requests.

For example, you might want to handle a GET request to /users by returning a list of users, and a POST request to /users by creating a new user.

Extracting Data from Requests

Besides extracting parameters from the URL, you can also extract data from other parts of the request, such as the headers or the request body. This allows you to access information that the client is sending to the server.

Real-World Examples

Routing and request handling are essential for building any web application:

- REST APIs: REST APIs use different routes and HTTP methods to expose different resources and actions.
- Single-page applications: Single-page applications often use routing to handle different views and states within the application.
- Content management systems: Content management systems use routing to display different pages and content based on the requested URL.

By mastering routing and request handling in hyper, you gain the ability to build sophisticated web applications that can handle a variety of requests and provide dynamic and interactive experiences for your users.

6.4 Serving Static Files

Let's make our web server a bit more useful! A common task for web servers is to serve static files, such as HTML pages, CSS stylesheets, JavaScript files, images, and other assets that make up a website. Think of it as your server acting as a librarian, retrieving files from its collection and handing them out to visitors (clients) upon request.

Serving static files efficiently is crucial for web performance. It allows users to quickly access the resources they need to view and interact with your website.

The tokio-fs Crate

While hyper provides the foundation for building web servers, it doesn't include built-in functionality for serving static files. However, we can leverage the power of the tokio-fs crate, which provides asynchronous file system operations, to seamlessly integrate file serving into our hyper server.

First, add tokio-fs to your Cargo.toml file:

Ini, TOML

```toml
[dependencies]

tokio-fs = "0.2" // Replace with the desired version
```

Serving Files with hyper

Now, let's modify our server to serve static files from a directory named "public":

Rust

```rust
use hyper::{Body, Request, Response, Server};

use hyper::service::{make_service_fn, service_fn};

use std::convert::Infallible;

use std::path::Path;

use tokio::fs::File;

use tokio::io::AsyncReadExt;

async fn handle_request(req: Request<Body>) -> Result<Response<Body>, Infallible> {

    let path = Path::new("public").join(req.uri().path().trim_start_matches('/'));
```

```rust
        let path = path.to_str().unwrap();
        match File::open(path).await {
            Ok(mut file) => {
                let mut contents = Vec::new();
                file.read_to_end(&mut contents).await.unwrap();
                let body = Body::from(contents);
                let response = Response::new(body);
                Ok(response)
            }
            Err(_) => {
                Ok(Response::builder()
                    .status(404)
                    .body(Body::from("Not Found"))
                    .unwrap())
            }
        }
    }
#[tokio::main]
async fn main() {
    // ... (server setup code) ...
```

}

In this example:

- We construct the file path by joining the "public" directory with the requested path from the URL.
- We use File::open(path) to open the file asynchronously.
- If the file exists, we read its contents into a Vec<u8> and create a response with those contents as the body.
- If the file doesn't exist, we return a 404 Not Found response.

Now, if you create a "public" directory in your project and place an index.html file in it, visiting http://127.0.0.1:3000 in your browser will serve the contents of that HTML file.

Content-Type Headers

For the browser to correctly interpret and display the served files, you should set the appropriate Content-Type header in the response. This header tells the browser what type of content it's receiving (e.g., text/html for HTML files, image/png for PNG images).

You can use libraries like mime_guess to determine the content type based on the file extension.

Real-World Examples

Serving static files is a fundamental aspect of web development:

- Websites: Websites are composed of various static files, such as HTML, CSS, JavaScript, and images, that are served by web servers.
- Web applications: Even dynamic web applications often rely on static files for their user interface and assets.

- File hosting services: Services like Dropbox and Google Drive allow users to store and share files, which are essentially served as static files.

Security Considerations

When serving static files, keep security in mind:

- Avoid serving sensitive files: Make sure that your server doesn't accidentally serve sensitive files, such as configuration files or private data.
- Prevent directory traversal attacks: Ensure that users cannot access files outside the designated public directory by manipulating the URL.

By mastering the techniques of serving static files with hyper and tokio-fs, you can build web servers that efficiently deliver the assets that make up your websites and applications. Remember to handle errors gracefully, set appropriate content-type headers, and consider security implications to ensure a smooth and secure experience for your users.

6.5 Handling Data with Templates

Alright, let's add some dynamism to our web server! While serving static files is essential, most web applications need to generate dynamic content that's tailored to each user or request. This is where templates come in handy.

Think of a template as a blueprint for creating web pages. It contains the basic structure of the page, with placeholders for dynamic content. When a user requests the page, the server fills in those placeholders with actual data, creating a personalized page for that user. It's like having a form letter with blanks that you fill in with specific details for each recipient.

Templating Engines in Rust

Rust offers several excellent templating engines that you can use to generate dynamic content:

- **Handlebars:** Handlebars is a popular and easy-to-use templating language that uses a simple syntax with curly braces ({{ }}) to embed dynamic data.
- **Tera:** Tera is another powerful templating engine that offers more advanced features, such as inheritance, filters, and macros.
- **Askama:** Askama is a template engine that emphasizes type safety and compile-time checks.

The choice of templating engine depends on your preferences and the complexity of your application.

Using Templates with hyper

Let's use the handlebars crate to demonstrate how to integrate templates with our hyper server. First, add handlebars to your Cargo.toml file:

Ini, TOML

```
[dependencies]

handlebars = "4.0" // Replace with the desired version
```

Now, let's create a simple template and use it to generate a dynamic web page:

Rust

```
use handlebars::Handlebars;

use hyper::{Body, Request, Response, Server};
```

```
use hyper::service::{make_service_fn,
service_fn};

use std::convert::Infallible;

async fn[1] handle_request(_req: Request<Body>) ->
Result<Response<Body>, Infallible>[2] {

    let mut handlebars = Handlebars::new();

    handlebars.register_template_string("hello",
"Hello, {{name}}!").unwrap();

    let data = serde_json::json!({

        "name": "Alice"

    });

    let body = handlebars.render("hello",
&data).unwrap();

    Ok(Response::new(Body::from(body)))

}

#[tokio::main]

async fn main() {

    // ... (server setup code) ...

}
```

In this example:

- We create a Handlebars instance and register a template string named "hello".

- We create a `serde_json::Value` representing the data we want to pass to the template.
- We use `handlebars.render("hello", &data)` to render the template with the provided data.
- We create a response with the rendered template as the body.

Now, if you visit http://127.0.0.1:3000 in your browser, you should see the personalized greeting "Hello, Alice!" displayed.

Real-World Examples

Templates are used extensively in web development to create dynamic and interactive web pages:

- E-commerce websites: E-commerce websites use templates to display product information, user accounts, and shopping carts.
- Social media platforms: Social media platforms use templates to display user profiles, posts, and news feeds.
- Content management systems: Content management systems use templates to generate web pages from content stored in a database.
- Blog platforms: Blog platforms use templates to display blog posts, comments, and other dynamic content.

Benefits of Using Templates

Templates offer several benefits for web development:

- Separation of concerns: Templates separate the presentation logic (HTML) from the application logic (Rust code), making your code cleaner and easier to maintain.
- Code reusability: You can reuse templates across different parts of your application, reducing code duplication.

- Dynamic content: Templates allow you to generate dynamic content based on user input, data from databases, or other sources.
- Improved maintainability: Updating the design or layout of your website becomes easier by modifying the templates.

By mastering the use of templates with hyper, you gain a powerful tool for building dynamic and engaging web applications. You can create personalized experiences for your users and efficiently generate web pages that adapt to different contexts and data.

Chapter 7: Advanced Concurrency Patterns

We've already touched on the basics of concurrency with threads, but Rust offers a rich set of tools and patterns for managing concurrent operations effectively. In this chapter, we'll explore some advanced concurrency patterns that are particularly useful in network programming.

Think of these patterns as sophisticated strategies for coordinating multiple tasks and managing shared resources in a concurrent environment. They're like advanced teamwork techniques that allow different parts of your application to work together seamlessly and efficiently.

7.1 Channels for Communication

Think of a channel as a pipeline that connects different parts of your application. You can send data down this pipeline from one end, and it will emerge at the other end, ready to be received and processed by another part of your application. It's like a secure and reliable communication channel between different teams in a company, allowing them to exchange information and coordinate their efforts without stepping on each other's toes.

Channels in Rust

Rust provides channels through the std::sync::mpsc module (mpsc stands for "multiple producer, single consumer"). This module allows you to create channels that can be used to send data between threads.

Here's a breakdown of how channels work:

- Creating a channel: You create a new channel using the mpsc::channel() function. This function returns a tuple (tx, rx), where tx is the sending end (transmitter) and rx is the receiving end (receiver).
- Sending data: To send data through the channel, you use the send() method on the transmitter (tx). This method takes the data you want to send as an argument and sends it down the channel.
- Receiving data: To receive data from the channel, you use the recv() method on the receiver (rx). This method blocks until data is available on the channel and then returns the received data.
- Ownership and move semantics: When you send data through a channel, ownership of the data is transferred to the receiver. This means that the sender can no longer access the data after it has been sent.

Example

Let's illustrate the use of channels with a simple example:

Rust

```rust
use std::sync::mpsc;

use std::thread;

fn main() {

    let (tx, rx) = mpsc::channel(); // Create a channel

    thread::spawn(move || {

        let message = String::from("Hello from the spawned thread!");
```

```
        tx.send(message).unwrap(); // Send a
message

    });

    let received = rx.recv().unwrap(); // Receive
the message

    println!("Received: {}", received); //
Output: Received: Hello from the spawned thread!

}
```

In this example:

- We create a new channel using mpsc::channel().
- We spawn a new thread that sends a message "Hello from the spawned thread!" through the tx transmitter.
- The main thread waits for a message on the rx receiver using rx.recv() and then prints the received message to the console.

Use Cases for Channels

Channels are incredibly versatile and can be used in various scenarios in network programming:

- Passing data between threads: Imagine a web server that receives requests from multiple clients. You can use channels to pass the request data from the thread handling the network connection to a worker thread that processes the request.
- Sending notifications: You can use channels to send notifications between threads. For example, a thread monitoring a network socket can send a notification to another thread when data is available to be read.

- Coordinating actions: Channels can be used to coordinate actions between threads. For instance, you can use a channel to signal that a task has been completed or to synchronize access to a shared resource.

Types of Channels

The std::sync::mpsc module provides different types of channels:

- channel(): Creates a basic channel with a single sender and a single receiver.
- sync_channel(): Creates a synchronous channel where the send() method blocks until the receiver is ready to receive the data.
- try_send() **and** try_recv(): These methods allow you to send and receive data without blocking.

Real-World Examples

Channels are used extensively in concurrent applications, including:

- Web servers: Web servers use channels to distribute incoming requests to worker threads.
- Operating systems: Operating systems use channels for inter-process communication.
- Concurrency libraries: Many concurrency libraries, such as rayon and crossbeam, use channels as a fundamental building block.

7.2 Shared State and Synchronization

When multiple threads or asynchronous tasks access and modify the same data concurrently, things can get tricky. Without proper coordination, you might encounter data races, where the outcome of your program becomes unpredictable and depends on the chaotic timing of thread execution.

Think of shared state as a whiteboard that multiple people can write on simultaneously. If everyone scribbles on the board without any rules or coordination, the result will be a jumbled mess of overlapping text and illegible scribbles. Synchronization is like establishing rules and protocols for who can write on the board when, ensuring that the information on the board remains organized, consistent, and accurate.

Need for Synchronization

In concurrent programs, synchronization is essential to:

- Prevent data races: Data races occur when multiple threads access and modify the same data without proper coordination. This can lead to unpredictable and incorrect behavior, as the final value of the data might depend on which thread "wins" the race to modify it last.
- Maintain data consistency: Synchronization ensures that shared data remains consistent and valid even when multiple threads are accessing and modifying it. This is crucial for preventing errors and ensuring the integrity of your application's data.
- Coordinate actions: Synchronization allows you to coordinate actions between threads, such as ensuring that one thread waits for another thread to complete a task before proceeding.

Mutexes in Rust

Rust provides a powerful tool for synchronization called a mutex (mutual exclusion). A mutex is like a lock that protects shared data. Only one thread can hold the lock at a time, ensuring that only one thread can access and modify the shared data at any given moment. It's like having a single key to a shared resource – only the key holder can access the resource at any given time.

The std::sync::Mutex type in Rust provides mutex functionality. Here's how you can use it:

Rust

```rust
use std::sync::{Arc, Mutex};

use std::thread;

fn main() {

    let counter = Arc::new(Mutex::new(0)); // Create a shared counter

    let mut handles = vec![];

    for _ in 0..10 {

        let counter = Arc::clone(&counter);

        let handle = thread::spawn(move || {

            let mut num = counter.lock().unwrap();[1] // Acquire the lock

            *num += 1; // Modify the shared data

        });

        handles.push(handle);

    }

    for handle in handles {

        handle.join().unwrap();

    }
```

```
    println!("Result: {}",
*counter.lock().unwrap()); // Output: Result: 10

}
```

In this example:

- We create a shared counter using Arc::new(Mutex::new(0)). Arc (atomic reference count) allows multiple threads to own the counter, and Mutex protects it from data races.
- We spawn 10 threads that each increment the counter.
- Each thread acquires the lock on the mutex using counter.lock().unwrap(). This blocks the thread until the lock is available.
- Once the lock is acquired, the thread can safely access and modify the shared counter.
- The lock is automatically released when the MutexGuard (returned by lock()) goes out of scope.

Other Synchronization Primitives

Besides mutexes, Rust provides other synchronization primitives for different scenarios:

- RWLock (reader-writer lock): Allows multiple readers or one writer to access shared data concurrently. This is useful when you have data that is frequently read but infrequently modified.
- Condvar (condition variable): Allows threads to wait for a specific condition to become true before proceeding. This is useful for coordinating actions between threads, such as signaling when data is available or a task has been completed.
- Atomic types: Provides lock-free, thread-safe operations on primitive data types. These are useful for simple operations that don't require complex synchronization.

Real-World Examples

Synchronization is crucial in various real-world concurrent applications:

- Databases: Databases use synchronization to ensure data consistency and prevent conflicts when multiple users access and modify data simultaneously.
- Operating systems: Operating systems use synchronization to manage access to shared resources, such as memory, files, and network interfaces.
- Game development: Game engines use synchronization to coordinate actions between different game entities and prevent race conditions that could lead to glitches or crashes.

7.3 Thread Pools and Work Stealing

When you have many tasks to execute concurrently, creating and managing individual threads for each task can become inefficient and cumbersome. Thread pools provide a more organized and efficient way to handle a pool of worker threads that can execute tasks as needed.

Think of a thread pool as a busy office with a group of employees ready to tackle tasks. When a new task arrives, it's assigned to an available employee. If all employees are busy, the task is added to a queue and waits for an employee to become free. This organized approach ensures that tasks are processed efficiently without the overhead of constantly creating and destroying threads.

How Thread Pools Work

A thread pool typically consists of:

- A queue of tasks: This queue holds the tasks that need to be executed.

- A pool of worker threads: These threads wait for tasks to become available in the queue.
- A manager: The manager is responsible for assigning tasks to worker threads and managing the pool's resources.

When a new task arrives, the manager adds it to the task queue. An available worker thread takes the task from the queue and executes it. Once the task is complete, the worker thread becomes available to take another task from the queue.

Benefits of Thread Pools

Thread pools offer several advantages:

- Reduced overhead: By reusing threads from the pool, you avoid the overhead of creating and destroying threads for each task. This can significantly improve performance, especially when dealing with many short-lived tasks.
- Controlled concurrency: Thread pools allow you to control the number of threads used, preventing your application from creating too many threads and overwhelming system resources.
- Simplified task management: Thread pools handle the complexities of thread management, allowing you to focus on defining and submitting tasks.

Work Stealing

Work stealing is a technique used in conjunction with thread pools to further improve efficiency. In a traditional thread pool, if one thread has a long-running task, other threads might become idle while waiting for new tasks. Work stealing allows idle threads to "steal" tasks from the queues of busy threads, ensuring that all threads are utilized effectively.

Think of it as a team of employees where someone who finishes their work early can offer to help a colleague who is still busy. This collaborative approach ensures that everyone is productive and no one is sitting idle.

Thread Pool Implementations in Rust

Rust provides several crates that offer thread pool implementations with work stealing capabilities:

- **threadpool**: This crate provides a basic thread pool implementation.
- **rayon**: This crate provides a more advanced thread pool with work stealing and data parallelism features. It's particularly well-suited for parallel computations.

Here's a simple example using the threadpool crate:

Rust

```rust
use threadpool::ThreadPool;

fn main() {
    let pool = ThreadPool::new(4); // Create a thread pool with 4 worker threads

    for i in 0..10 {
        pool.execute(move || {
            println!("Task {} executed by worker thread", i);

            // ... perform some work ...
        });
    }
}
```

```
    pool.join(); // Wait for all tasks to
complete
```

}

In this example, we create a thread pool with 4 worker threads and submit 10 tasks to the pool. The execute() method adds a task to the pool's queue, and the join() method waits for all tasks to complete.

Real-World Examples

Thread pools are used in various applications:

- Web servers: Web servers use thread pools to handle concurrent requests from clients.
- Operating systems: Operating systems use thread pools to manage system tasks and background processes.
- Game development: Game engines use thread pools to execute game logic, physics simulations, and rendering tasks concurrently.

By understanding and utilizing thread pools and work stealing, you can efficiently manage concurrency in your Rust applications, especially when dealing with a large number of tasks or computationally intensive operations.

7.4 Asynchronous Streams

In network programming, you often encounter situations where data arrives in chunks or over a period of time, rather than all at once. Asynchronous streams provide an elegant way to process this data as it becomes available without blocking the execution of other tasks.

Think of an asynchronous stream as a conveyor belt that delivers items one by one. You can process each item as it arrives on the belt, without having to wait for the entire belt to be filled. This "on-demand" processing is particularly useful in network applications where data might arrive in bursts or at unpredictable intervals.

The Stream Trait in Tokio

Tokio provides the Stream trait for working with asynchronous streams. This trait defines methods for asynchronously iterating over the items in a stream. It's like having a special iterator that can pause and resume as needed, allowing other tasks to execute while waiting for the next item in the stream.

The key method of the Stream trait is poll_next(). This method attempts to retrieve the next item from the stream. If an item is available, it returns Poll::Ready(Some(item)). If the stream has ended, it returns Poll::Ready(None). If the stream is not yet ready with an item, it returns Poll::Pending, allowing other tasks to execute.

Creating Asynchronous Streams

There are several ways to create asynchronous streams in Tokio:

- From iterators: You can convert a synchronous iterator into an asynchronous stream using the stream::iter() function.
- From futures: You can create a stream that yields a single item from a future using the stream::once() function.
- From channels: You can create a stream from the receiver end of a channel using the stream::channel() function. This allows you to receive data asynchronously from other parts of your application.
- Custom implementations: You can implement the Stream trait yourself to create custom streams that generate data according to your specific needs.

Working with Asynchronous Streams

Once you have an asynchronous stream, you can use for_each() to process each item in the stream concurrently:

Rust

```
use tokio::stream::{self, StreamExt};

#[tokio::main]
async fn main() {
    let stream = stream::iter(vec![1, 2, 3]);
    stream
        .for_each(|item| async move {
            println!("Got item: {}", item);
            // ... process the item ...
        })
        .await;
}
```

In this example, we create a stream from a vector and use for_each() to print each item in the stream. The async move block allows us to perform asynchronous operations within the for_each() closure.

Real-World Examples

Asynchronous streams are used in various network applications:

- Reading data from a socket: You can create an asynchronous stream that yields chunks of data as they are received from a network socket.
- Processing real-time data: You can use asynchronous streams to process real-time data from sensors, financial markets, or other sources.
- Streaming APIs: Many web APIs provide data as asynchronous streams, allowing clients to process data as it arrives without having to wait for the entire response.

Benefits of Asynchronous Streams

Asynchronous streams offer several benefits:

- Non-blocking: They allow you to process data as it becomes available without blocking the execution of other tasks.
- Efficiency: They can efficiently handle streams of data that arrive in chunks or at unpredictable intervals.
- Composability: You can combine asynchronous streams with other asynchronous operations, such as futures and tasks, to create complex concurrent workflows.

By understanding and utilizing asynchronous streams, you can build highly efficient and responsive network applications that can handle dynamic data flows and process information in a non-blocking manner. They are a powerful tool for managing concurrency and building real-time applications in Rust.

Chapter 8: Network Security

Network security is a critical aspect of any network application, especially those handling sensitive data or providing essential services. Think of it as adding strong locks and security systems to your house to protect your valuable belongings and ensure the safety of your family.

In this chapter, we'll explore essential network security concepts and learn how to implement them in our Rust applications. We'll cover topics like Transport Layer Security (TLS), encryption and decryption, and authentication and authorization.

8.1 Transport Layer Security

Think of TLS as establishing a secure tunnel between your application and the server you're communicating with. This tunnel ensures that any data exchanged between them remains confidential and protected from prying eyes, eavesdropping, or tampering. It's like having a private conversation in a crowded room, where only you and the intended recipient can understand what's being said.

TLS, and its predecessor Secure Sockets Layer (SSL), is a cryptographic protocol that provides secure communication over a network. It's a widely adopted standard used to secure various internet services, including:

- Web browsing (HTTPS): TLS is used to secure communication between web browsers and web servers, protecting sensitive information like passwords, credit card details, and personal data during online transactions and interactions.

- Email communication: TLS is used to secure email transmission, preventing unauthorized access to your emails and ensuring their confidentiality.
- VPN (Virtual Private Network): TLS is often used in VPNs to create secure connections between your device and a remote server, protecting your internet traffic from eavesdropping and censorship.
- File transfer: TLS can be used to secure file transfers, ensuring that files are transmitted confidentially and without tampering.

How TLS Works

TLS uses a combination of cryptographic techniques to achieve secure communication:

- Encryption: TLS encrypts the data exchanged between the client and the server using strong encryption algorithms. This makes the data unreadable to anyone who intercepts the communication, even if they can capture the network traffic.
- Authentication: TLS allows the client and server to verify each other's identities using digital certificates. This ensures that you're communicating with the intended party and not an imposter trying to steal your information.
- Integrity: TLS uses message authentication codes (MACs) to ensure that the data exchanged between the client and server has not been tampered with during transmission. This guarantees that the data you receive is the same as the data that was sent.

TLS typically operates on top of TCP, adding a layer of security to the reliable transport protocol. It uses a handshake process to establish a secure connection, during which the client and server negotiate the encryption algorithms, exchange keys, and verify certificates.

TLS in Rust

Rust provides excellent support for TLS through crates like rustls and openssl. These crates provide implementations of the TLS protocol, allowing you to easily integrate TLS into your network applications.

Here's a simple example using rustls to create a secure TCP client:

Rust

```rust
use rustls::ClientConfig;

use std::io::{BufReader, BufWriter};

use std::net::TcpStream;

use std::sync::Arc;

use tokio::io::{AsyncReadExt, AsyncWriteExt};

use tokio::net::TcpStream as TokioTcpStream;

#[tokio::main]

async fn main() {

    let mut config = ClientConfig::new();

    config

        .root_store


.add_server_trust_anchors(&webpki_roots::TLS_SERVER_ROOTS);

    let config = Arc::new(config);
```

```
    let¹ stream =
TokioTcpStream::connect("google.com:443").await.u
nwrap();

    let mut stream =
rustls::ClientConnection::new(config,
"google.com".try_into().unwrap())

        .unwrap()

        .into_io(stream)

        .unwrap();

    stream.write_all(b"GET /
HTTP/1.1\r\n\r\n").await.unwrap();

    let mut reader = BufReader::new(stream);

    let mut buffer = String::new();

    reader.read_to_string(&mut buffer).unwrap();

    println!("{}", buffer);

}
```

In this example:

- We create a ClientConfig for TLS and add the necessary root certificates for trust anchors.
- We established a TCP connection to google.com:443.
- We create a ClientConnection using rustls to secure the connection.
- We send an HTTP request over the secure connection and receive the response.

Benefits of TLS

TLS provides numerous benefits for network security:

- Confidentiality: TLS encrypts data, protecting it from unauthorized access.
- Integrity: TLS ensures data integrity, preventing tampering during transmission.
- Authentication: TLS verifies the identity of the server, preventing man-in-the-middle attacks.
- Trust: TLS establishes trust between the client and the server, ensuring secure communication.

By understanding and utilizing TLS in your Rust applications, you can significantly enhance their security and protect sensitive data during network communication.

8.2 Encryption and Decryption

In network programming, encryption is crucial for protecting data as it travels across the network. Whether it's passwords, financial information, personal messages, or confidential documents, encryption ensures that even if someone intercepts the data, they won't be able to understand or misuse it.

How Encryption Works

Encryption involves transforming data into an unreadable format using an encryption algorithm and a secret key. This transformed data is called ciphertext. Decryption is the reverse process, where the ciphertext is converted back into its original form (plaintext) using the same or a related key.

Think of it as putting your message in a box and locking it with a key. Only someone with the same key can unlock the box and read the message.

Types of Encryption

There are two main types of encryption:

- **Symmetric encryption:** Uses the same key for both encryption and decryption. It's like having one key that can both lock and unlock the box. Symmetric encryption is generally faster and more efficient but requires a secure way to share the key between the sender and receiver.
- **Asymmetric encryption:** Uses different keys for encryption and decryption: a public key and a private key. The public key can be freely shared with anyone,[1] while the private key must be kept secret.[2] Data encrypted with the public key can only be decrypted with the corresponding private key. It's like having two keys: one to lock the box (public key) and another to unlock it (private key). Asymmetric encryption is more complex but provides a secure way to exchange keys and establish secure communication channels.

Encryption Algorithms

There are numerous encryption algorithms available, each with its own strengths and weaknesses. Some common algorithms include:

- **AES (Advanced Encryption Standard):** A widely used symmetric encryption algorithm that provides strong security and efficient performance.
- **RSA (Rivest-Shamir-Adleman):** A widely used asymmetric encryption algorithm that's often used for key exchange and digital signatures.
- **ChaCha20-Poly1305:** A modern stream cipher that offers high performance and security.

The choice of encryption algorithm depends on various factors, such as the level of security required, performance considerations, and compatibility with other systems.

Encryption in Rust

Rust provides several crates that offer implementations of various encryption algorithms:

- aes-gcm: Provides an implementation of the AES-GCM encryption algorithm.
- rsa: Provides an implementation of the RSA encryption algorithm.
- sodiumoxide: Provides bindings to the libsodium library, which offers a wide range of cryptographic primitives, including encryption algorithms.

Here's a simple example using the aes-gcm crate to encrypt and decrypt data:

Rust

```rust
use aes_gcm::{
    aead::{Aead, NewAead},
    Aes256Gcm, Key, Nonce, // Or `Aes128Gcm`
};

fn main() {
    let key = Key::from_slice(b"an example very very secret key."); // 32-bytes
    let cipher = Aes256Gcm::new(key);
```

```
    let nonce = Nonce::from_slice(b"unique nonce"); // 96-bits; unique per message

    let ciphertext = cipher
        .encrypt(nonce,[3] b"plaintext message".as_ref())
        .expect("encryption failure!"); // NOTE: handle this error to avoid panics!

    let plaintext = cipher
        .decrypt(nonce, ciphertext.as_ref())
        .expect("decryption failure!"); // NOTE: handle this error to avoid panics!

    assert_eq!(&plaintext, b"plaintext message");[4]

}
```

In this example, we create an instance of the Aes256Gcm cipher, encrypt a plaintext message using a key and nonce, and then decrypt the ciphertext back to the original plaintext.

Real-World Examples

Encryption is used extensively in various applications and systems:

- Secure communication: TLS/SSL uses encryption to secure communication between web browsers and web servers, email clients and mail servers, and other network applications.
- Data protection: Encryption is used to protect sensitive data stored on devices and in databases, such as passwords, credit card information, and medical records.

- Digital signatures: Asymmetric encryption is used to create digital signatures, which verify the authenticity and integrity of digital documents.
- Virtual private networks (VPNs): VPNs use encryption to secure internet traffic and protect user privacy.

8.3 Authentication and Authorization

These two are like the gatekeepers of your application, ensuring that only authorized users can access specific resources or perform certain actions.

Think of it like entering a secure building. Authentication is like showing your ID card to the security guard to prove your identity. Authorization is like the guard checking your access level to determine which areas of the building you're allowed to enter.

In network applications, authentication and authorization are essential for protecting sensitive data and ensuring that only legitimate users can access specific functionalities.

Authentication: Verifying Identity

Authentication is the process of verifying the identity of a user or device. It's like confirming that someone is who they claim to be. In network applications, authentication is typically used to verify the identity of users before granting them access to the application or its resources.

There are various methods for authentication, each with its own strengths and weaknesses:

- Passwords: Users provide a password that's compared to a stored hash of the password. This is a common and simple method but can be vulnerable to attacks if passwords are weak or stored insecurely.

- Tokens: Users provide a token, which is a string of characters that acts as a temporary credential. Tokens can be generated by the server and sent to the client after successful authentication. This approach is often used in web applications and APIs.
- Biometrics: Users authenticate using unique biological traits, such as fingerprints, facial recognition, or voice recognition. This method provides strong security but requires specialized hardware and software.
- Multi-factor authentication (MFA): Combines multiple authentication methods for increased security. For example, a user might need to provide both a password and a one-time code sent to their phone.

Authorization: Granting Access

Authorization is the process of determining what actions an authenticated user or device is allowed to perform. It's like checking someone's permissions or access level to decide what they're allowed to do.

Authorization often involves checking roles and permissions:

- Roles: Users are assigned roles (e.g., administrator, editor, viewer), and each role has specific permissions. This allows you to group users with similar access levels and manage their permissions collectively.
- Permissions: Permissions define what actions a user is allowed to perform on specific resources (e.g., read, write, delete). This provides fine-grained control over access to sensitive data and functionalities.

Authentication and Authorization in Rust

Rust provides several crates that offer tools for implementing authentication and authorization in your applications:

- **jsonwebtoken:** Provides tools for creating and verifying JSON Web Tokens (JWTs), which are commonly used for authentication in web applications and APIs.
- **actix-web-httpauth:** Provides middleware for authentication and authorization in Actix Web applications.
- **oauth2:** Provides support for OAuth 2.0, a popular authorization framework used by many web services.

Here's a simple example using jsonwebtoken to create and verify a JWT:

```Rust
use jsonwebtoken::{encode, decode, Header, Validation, EncodingKey};

use serde::{Serialize, Deserialize};

#[derive(Debug, Serialize, Deserialize)]
struct Claims {
    sub: String,
    company: String,
    exp: usize,
}

fn main() {
    let my_claims = Claims {
        sub: "b@b.com".to_owned(),
        company: "ACME".to_owned(),
        exp: 10000000000,
```

```rust
    };

    let key =
EncodingKey::from_secret("secret".as_ref());

    let token = encode(&Header::default(),
&my_claims, &key).unwrap();

    println!("Token: {}", token);

    let token_data = decode::<Claims>(&token,
&DecodingKey::from_secret("secret".as_ref()),
&Validation::new(Algorithm::HS256)).unwrap();

    println!("Token data: {:?}", token_data);

}
```

In this example, we create a JWT containing some claims (user information) and then decode the token to verify its authenticity and extract the claims.

Real-World Examples

Authentication and authorization are used in almost every application that requires user accounts or access control:

- Web applications: Web applications use authentication to verify user logins and authorization to control access to different parts of the application, such as user profiles, admin panels, or paid content.
- APIs: APIs use authentication to verify the identity of clients and authorization to control access to different API endpoints and resources.
- Operating systems: Operating systems use authentication to verify user logins and authorization to control access to files, directories, and system resources.

- Cloud services: Cloud services use authentication and authorization to control access to cloud resources, such as virtual machines, storage buckets, and databases.

By implementing robust authentication and authorization mechanisms in your Rust applications, you can ensure that only authorized users can access sensitive data and perform specific actions, enhancing the security and trustworthiness of your applications.

Chapter 9: Building a Real-time Chat Application

Imagine creating a platform where users can connect and exchange messages instantly, just like popular messaging apps we use every day. This is where the power of WebSockets comes into play.

In this chapter, we'll learn how to build a real-time chat application in Rust using WebSockets. We'll explore how WebSockets enable bi-directional communication, handle multiple users and chat rooms, and broadcast messages efficiently.

9.1 WebSockets

WebSockets is a powerful communication protocol that opens up a whole new dimension of possibilities for building interactive and engaging network applications. Think of WebSockets as a direct line of communication between your application and a server, enabling real-time, two-way data exchange.

Traditional web communication relies on the HTTP protocol, which follows a request-response pattern. The client sends a request to the server, the server processes the request and sends back a response, and then the connection is closed. This works well for many web interactions, but it falls short when you need real-time, continuous communication.

Imagine you're building a chat application. With HTTP, each message would require a separate request and response, creating a lot of overhead and latency. WebSockets, on the other hand, establishes a persistent connection between the client and the server. Once the connection is established, both parties can send data back and forth at any time, creating a seamless and responsive experience.

How WebSockets Work

WebSockets start with an HTTP handshake, which is like a polite introduction between the client and the server. During this handshake, the client requests an upgrade to the WebSocket protocol, and the server agrees if it supports WebSockets.

Once the handshake is successful, the connection is upgraded to a WebSocket connection, and a persistent, bi-directional communication channel is established. This means that both the client and the server can send data to each other at any time, without having to initiate new requests.

Key Features of WebSockets

- Bi-directional communication: Both the client and the server can send data to each other, enabling real-time interactions and updates.
- Full-duplex communication: Data can flow in both directions simultaneously, without interrupting the flow in either direction.
- Low latency: WebSockets are designed for low-latency communication, making them ideal for applications where responsiveness is crucial.
- Persistent connection: The connection remains open until explicitly closed by either the client or the server, reducing overhead and enabling efficient data transfer.

Real-World Examples

WebSockets are used in a wide variety of applications where real-time communication is essential:

- Chat applications: Popular messaging apps like Slack, Discord, and WhatsApp use WebSockets to enable instant messaging.

- Online games: Multiplayer online games rely on WebSockets to synchronize game state, player actions, and chat messages between players and the game server.
- Collaborative tools: Collaborative editing tools like Google Docs use WebSockets to allow multiple users to edit the same document simultaneously.
- Financial trading platforms: Financial trading platforms use WebSockets to provide real-time market data and enable traders to execute trades instantly.
- IoT (Internet of Things): IoT devices often use WebSockets to communicate with cloud servers and provide real-time updates on sensor data or device status.

WebSockets in Rust

Rust provides several crates for working with WebSockets, including:

- tokio-tungstenite: This crate provides a Tokio-based implementation of the WebSocket protocol, allowing you to create WebSocket servers and clients within the Tokio runtime.
- warp: This crate provides a web framework that includes support for WebSockets, making it easy to integrate WebSockets into your web applications.

Here's a simple example using tokio-tungstenite to create a WebSocket echo server:

Rust

```
use std::net::SocketAddr;

use tokio_tungstenite::connect_async;
```

```
use tokio_tungstenite::tungstenite::Message;

#[tokio::main]

async fn main() {

    let url =
url::Url::parse("ws://127.0.0.1:9001").unwrap();

    let (ws_stream, _) =
connect_async(url).await.expect("Failed to
connect");

    println!("Connected to the server");

    let (write, read) = ws_stream.split();[1]

    tokio::spawn(async move {

        for msg in read {

            println!("Received: {}",
msg.unwrap());

        }

    });

    write.send(Message::Text("Hello
WebSocket".into())).await.unwrap();

}
```

In this example:

- We establish a WebSocket connection to the server at the specified URL.
- We split the WebSocket stream into a write half (write) and a read half (read).

- We spawn a separate task to handle incoming messages on the `read` half.
- We send a text message "Hello WebSocket" to the server using the `write` half.

By understanding and utilizing WebSockets in your Rust applications, you can unlock the power of real-time communication and build interactive and engaging experiences for your users.

9.2 Handling Multiple Users and Chat Rooms

Let's tackle the challenge of building a chat application that can handle multiple users connecting, chatting, and potentially participating in different chat rooms. This involves managing connections, tracking users, and routing messages efficiently. Think of it as building a virtual coffee shop where people can come and go, engage in conversations, and move between different tables (chat rooms) as they please.

Managing Connections

When a user connects to your chat server via a WebSocket, you need a way to keep track of their connection. This is essential for sending messages to the correct users and managing resources effectively.

A common approach is to use a `HashMap` to store active WebSocket connections. You can use a unique identifier, such as a user ID or a randomly generated session ID, as the key and the WebSocket sender as the value.

Rust

```
use std::collections::HashMap;
```

```rust
use tokio::sync::mpsc;

// ... other imports ...

type Tx = mpsc::UnboundedSender<Message>;

struct ChatServer {

    connections: HashMap<usize, Tx>,

    // ... other fields ...

}
```

In this example, connections is a HashMap that stores the active WebSocket connections. The key is a usize representing the user ID, and the value is the Tx (transmitter) end of a channel that can be used to send messages to that user's WebSocket connection.

When a new user connects, you generate a unique ID for them, create a channel to communicate with their WebSocket, and add their ID and transmitter to the connections map. When a user disconnects, you remove their entry from the map.

Handling Chat Rooms

To support chat rooms, you need a way to group users and ensure that messages are only delivered to users in the same room. You can use another HashMap to store chat rooms, where the key is the room name and the value is a set of user IDs present in that room.

Rust

```rust
struct ChatServer {

    // ... other fields ...

    rooms: HashMap<String, HashSet<usize>>,
```

}

When a user joins a chat room, you add their ID to the set of users in that room. When a user leaves a room, you remove their ID from the set.

Routing Messages

When a user sends a message, you need to determine which users should receive it. If the message is sent to a specific chat room, you iterate over the users in that room and send the message to each of them. If the message is a private message to another user, you look up the recipient's ID in the connection map and send the message directly to their WebSocket.

Example: Code Snippet

```rust
// ... inside the ChatServer struct ...

async fn handle_message(&mut self, user_id: usize, message: Message) {
    // ... parse the message to determine the target (room or user) ...

    if let Some(room_name) = message.target_room {
        // Send the message to all users in the room
        if let Some(users) = self.rooms.get(&room_name) {
            for &user_id in users {
```

```
            if let Some(tx) = self.connections.get(&user_id) {
                    // Send the message using the tx channel
                }
            }
        }
    } else if let Some(recipient_id) = message.target_user {
        // Send the message to the specific user
        if let Some(tx) = self.connections.get(&recipient_id) {
            // Send the message using the tx channel
        }
    }
}
```

Real-World Examples

Handling multiple users and chat rooms is essential for any chat application:

- Slack: Slack allows users to create and join different channels (chat rooms) for organized communication within teams and communities.
- Discord: Discord provides servers with multiple channels for text and voice communication, allowing users to join

different communities and participate in various discussions.
- Online games: Many online games have chat functionalities that allow players to communicate with each other in different channels or within specific game areas.

By effectively managing connections, handling chat rooms, and routing messages, you can build robust and scalable chat applications that provide a seamless and engaging experience for multiple users.

9.3 Broadcasting Messages

Broadcasting is like making an announcement to a group of people. In a chat context, it involves sending a message to multiple recipients simultaneously, such as all users in a chat room or all online users.

Think of it like a town square where a speaker addresses a crowd. The speaker's voice reaches everyone in the square at the same time, delivering the same message to all listeners. Similarly, broadcasting in a chat application allows you to efficiently distribute messages to multiple recipients.

How Broadcasting Works

In our chat application, we can implement broadcasting by iterating over the active WebSocket connections and sending the message to each connection's corresponding sender.

Here's a simplified example:

```rust
// ... inside the ChatServer struct ...
```

```rust
async fn broadcast_message(&self, room_name: &str, message: &str) {
    if let Some(users) = self.rooms.get(room_name) {
        for &user_id in users {
            if let Some(tx) = self.connections.get(&user_id) {
                if let Err(e) = tx.send(Message::Text(message.to_owned())) {
                    println!("Error sending message to user {}: {}", user_id, e);
                    // Handle the error, e.g., remove the user from the room
                }
            }
        }
    }
}
```

In this example:

- We retrieve the set of users in the specified room from the rooms map.
- We iterate over the user IDs in the set.
- For each user ID, we retrieve the corresponding transmitter (tx) from the connections map.
- We send the message to the user's WebSocket connection using the tx.send() method.

- We include error handling to gracefully handle situations where sending the message fails (e.g., if the user has disconnected).

Efficient Broadcasting

For chat applications with a large number of users, broadcasting messages efficiently becomes crucial. Sending individual messages to each user can put a significant load on the server and potentially cause delays.

To improve efficiency, consider these techniques:

- Message queues: Instead of sending messages directly to each user, you can use a message queue to buffer messages and distribute them to users asynchronously. This can help reduce the load on the server and improve responsiveness.
- Publish-subscribe systems: Publish-subscribe systems allow clients to subscribe to specific topics or channels. When a message is published to a topic, it's automatically delivered to all subscribers. This can be more efficient than iterating over all connections, especially when users are interested in different subsets of messages.

Real-World Examples

Broadcasting is used in various applications:

- Chat applications: Chat applications use broadcasting to send messages to all users in a chat room or to notify users of events, such as new user joining or a user leaving.
- Online games: Online games use broadcasting to update game state, send notifications to players, or announce events within the game world.
- Social media platforms: Social media platforms use broadcasting to deliver notifications to users about new posts, comments, or friend requests.

- Streaming services: Streaming services use broadcasting to deliver live video or audio streams to multiple viewers simultaneously.

By understanding and implementing broadcasting techniques in your Rust chat application, you can efficiently distribute messages to multiple users, creating a responsive and engaging real-time communication experience.

Chapter 10: Performance Optimization

Think of performance optimization as fine-tuning a race car. Every component, from the engine to the tires, needs to be optimized to achieve maximum speed and efficiency. Similarly, in network programming, we need to carefully consider various factors to ensure our applications perform at their best.

In this chapter, we'll explore techniques for optimizing the performance of our Rust network applications. We'll cover profiling and benchmarking, buffering strategies, multiplexing and I/O models, and zero-copy networking.

10.1 Profiling and Benchmarking

Profiling and benchmarking are essential tools in a performance optimizer's toolbox. They help us measure and analyze our code's performance, pinpoint areas that need attention, and track the impact of our optimization efforts.

Profiling

Profiling is like taking your application to a doctor for a thorough check-up. It involves running your code and collecting data about its execution, such as how much time is spent in each function, how often specific lines of code are executed, and how much memory is allocated.

This data helps you identify performance hotspots – areas where your code is spending a significant amount of time or resources. By focusing your optimization efforts on these hotspots, you can achieve the most significant performance gains.

Profiling Tools in Rust

Rust offers a variety of profiling tools to help you analyze your code's performance:

- perf: This is a powerful command-line tool that comes with most Linux distributions. It allows you to collect performance data at a very low level, including CPU usage, cache misses, and branch mispredictions. You can use perf to profile your Rust applications and get detailed insights into their performance characteristics.
- Flamegraphs: Flamegraphs are visualizations of profiling data that show the call stack of your program and the amount of time spent in each function. They provide a clear and intuitive way to identify performance bottlenecks. Several crates, such as flamegraph and inferno, can generate flame graphs for your Rust applications.
- Profiling crates: Several Rust crates provide programmatic access to profiling data. For example, the cpuprofiler crate allows you to collect CPU profiling data and generate reports.

Benchmarking

Benchmarking is like putting your application through a series of tests to measure its performance under different conditions. It involves running specific code sections or functionalities repeatedly and measuring the time it takes to execute them.

Rust provides built-in support for benchmarking with the #[bench] attribute in the test crate. This attribute allows you to write benchmark functions that measure the execution time of your code.

Here's a simple example:

```
Rust
```

```rust
#![feature(test)]

extern crate test;

use test::Bencher;

#[bench]
fn bench_my_function(b: &mut Bencher) {

    b.iter(|| {

        // Code to be benchmarked

    });

}
```

In this example, the bench_my_function function is marked with the #[bench] attribute, indicating that it's a benchmark function. The b.iter(|| { ... }) block runs the code to be benchmarked repeatedly, and the test measures the execution time.

Why Profile and Benchmark?

Profiling and benchmarking are essential for performance optimization because they:

- Identify bottlenecks: They help you pinpoint the areas in your code that are causing performance issues.
- Measure improvements: They allow you to measure the impact of your optimization efforts and see if they are actually improving performance.
- Compare alternatives: They help you compare different approaches or algorithms to see which one performs better.
- Track regressions: They can help you detect performance regressions (when code changes inadvertently worsen

performance) and ensure that your application maintains its speed and efficiency over time.

Real-World Examples

Profiling and benchmarking are used extensively in various software development scenarios:

- Game development: Game developers use profiling to identify performance bottlenecks in their game engines and optimize rendering, physics simulations, and game logic.
- Web servers: Web server developers use benchmarking to measure the throughput and latency of their servers under different loads and optimize their code to handle high traffic efficiently.
- Database systems: Database developers use profiling and benchmarking to optimize query performance and ensure that databases can handle large datasets and complex queries efficiently.

Incorporating profiling and benchmarking into your development workflow, you can gain valuable insights into your code's performance and make informed decisions about how to optimize it. This will help you create network applications that are not only functional but also fast, efficient, and responsive.

10.2 Buffering Strategies

Buffering is a powerful technique for optimizing performance in network applications. Think of a buffer as a temporary storage area, like a warehouse that holds goods before they are shipped out. In network programming, buffers are used to store data in memory before it's sent over the network or after it's received from the network.

Why is buffering so important for performance? Well, network operations can be relatively slow compared to operations in memory. By buffering data, you can reduce the number of times you need to interact with the network, which can significantly improve the speed and efficiency of your application.

How Buffering Works

When you send data over a network, the data needs to be copied from your application's memory to the operating system's network buffers before it can be transmitted. Similarly, when you receive data from the network, the data is first copied into the operating system's buffers and then copied to your application's memory.

Buffering allows you to control this data flow and optimize it for better performance. Instead of sending or receiving data in small chunks, you can accumulate data in a buffer and then send or receive it in larger chunks, reducing the overhead of interacting with the network.

Benefits of Buffering

Buffering offers several benefits for network applications:

- Reduced system calls: Each network operation typically involves a system call, which is a relatively expensive operation. By buffering data, you can reduce the number of system calls required to send or receive data, improving performance.
- Improved throughput: Buffering can help improve data transfer throughput by allowing you to send or receive data in larger chunks. This is because larger chunks of data can be transmitted more efficiently over the network.
- Smoother data flow: Buffering can help smooth out bursts of data, preventing congestion and improving the responsiveness of your application. If data arrives in bursts,

the buffer can absorb the bursts and release the data at a more consistent rate.

Buffering Strategies

There are different buffering strategies you can employ, each with its own trade-offs:

- Fixed-size buffers: You allocate a buffer of a fixed size. This is simple to implement but can be inefficient if the amount of data varies significantly.
- Dynamic buffers: You start with a small buffer and dynamically increase its size as needed. This can be more efficient than fixed-size buffers but adds complexity to memory management.
- Circular buffers: A circular buffer is a fixed-size buffer that wraps around when it reaches the end. This can be efficient for managing a continuous stream of data.

The choice of buffering strategy depends on the specific needs of your application, the characteristics of the data being transferred, and the performance requirements.

Buffering in Rust

Rust provides several ways to implement buffering:

- `Vec<u8>`: You can use a `Vec<u8>` as a dynamic buffer to store data.
- `BytesMut`: The `BytesMut` type from the `bytes` crate provides a mutable buffer that can be efficiently resized and manipulated.
- Custom buffers: You can implement your own custom buffer types using arrays or other data structures.

Real-World Examples

Buffering is used extensively in various network applications:

- Web servers: Web servers use buffering to efficiently handle requests and responses, especially when dealing with large files or high traffic.
- Streaming services: Streaming services use buffering to smooth out the delivery of video or audio content, preventing interruptions and providing a better user experience.
- Game clients and servers: Online games use buffering to handle network traffic and ensure smooth gameplay, even with varying network conditions.
- Database systems: Databases use buffering to improve query performance and reduce disk I/O.

Understanding and implementing appropriate buffering strategies in your Rust network applications, you can significantly improve their performance, efficiency, and responsiveness.

10.3 Multiplexing and I/O Models

This is a key technique that allows a single thread to manage multiple network connections concurrently: multiplexing. Think of it as a skilled receptionist who can handle multiple phone calls simultaneously, effortlessly switching between conversations without dropping any calls. In network programming, multiplexing enables a single thread to juggle multiple network connections, improving efficiency and scalability.

Challenges of Concurrent Connections

In network applications, you often need to handle multiple clients connecting and interacting with your server simultaneously. A naive approach would be to create a separate thread for each client connection. However, this can quickly become inefficient as the number of clients grows, leading to excessive resource consumption and context switching overhead.

Multiplexing offers a more elegant solution. It allows a single thread to monitor multiple network connections and efficiently handle events from those connections as they occur.

I/O Models

Before we dive into multiplexing, let's understand different I/O models that provide different approaches to handling network operations:

- Blocking I/O: This is the simplest model. When a thread performs an I/O operation, such as reading from a socket, it blocks (waits) until the operation is complete. It's like waiting in line at the bank – you can't do anything else until you're served.
- Non-blocking I/O: In this model, the thread doesn't block when performing an I/O operation. If the operation cannot be completed immediately, the system call returns an error, and the thread can continue executing other tasks. It's like checking if the bank teller is free. If they are, you get served; otherwise, you can come back later.
- I/O Multiplexing: This model allows a single thread to monitor multiple I/O operations, such as reading from multiple sockets. The thread blocks until at least one of the operations is ready to be completed. It's like waiting in a waiting area where you can read a book or do other things until your number is called.
- Asynchronous I/O: In this model, the thread initiates an I/O operation and continues executing other tasks. The operating system notifies the thread when the operation is complete. It's like giving your phone number to the bank teller and having them call you when they're ready to serve you.

Multiplexing with select, poll, and epoll

Multiplexing is typically implemented using system calls like select, poll, or epoll (on Linux). These system calls allow a thread to monitor multiple file descriptors (which can represent sockets, files, or other I/O resources) and be notified when any of them are ready for reading or writing.

- select: This is the oldest and most basic multiplexing system call. It allows you to monitor a set of file descriptors and block until one or more of them are ready.
- poll: This is similar to select but uses a different data structure to represent the file descriptors.
- epoll: This is a more efficient multiplexing system call available on Linux. It uses an event-driven approach, where the operating system notifies the thread only when a file descriptor becomes ready, reducing the overhead of polling.

Tokio and I/O Multiplexing

Tokio, the asynchronous runtime we've been using, utilizes an I/O multiplexing model based on epoll (on Linux) or kqueue (on macOS). This allows Tokio to efficiently handle thousands of concurrent connections on a single thread.

Real-World Examples

Multiplexing is used extensively in high-performance network applications:

- Web servers: Web servers like Nginx and Apache use multiplexing to handle thousands of concurrent client connections efficiently.
- Database servers: Database servers use multiplexing to manage connections from multiple clients and handle queries concurrently.

- Networking libraries: Many networking libraries, such as libuv (used by Node.js) and Boost.Asio (used in C++), utilize multiplexing to provide efficient asynchronous I/O operations.

Understanding multiplexing and I/O models, you gain valuable insights into how high-performance network applications manage concurrency and handle multiple connections efficiently. This knowledge will help you design and build scalable and responsive network applications in Rust.

10.4 Zero-Copy Networking

Zero-copy networking is a technique that can significantly boost the performance of our network applications. This technique aims to minimize the overhead of copying data between the application's memory and the operating system's kernel space during network operations.

Think of it like this: imagine you need to send a package to a friend. Instead of going to the post office, packaging the item, and having the post office deliver it, you could simply hand the package directly to your friend. That's essentially what zero-copy networking does – it eliminates the middleman (the copying of data) and allows data to be transferred directly from the source to the destination.

Overhead of Data Copying

In traditional network programming, when you send data over a network, the data needs to be copied multiple times:

1. **Application to kernel:** The data is copied from the application's memory space to the operating system's kernel space.
2. **Kernel to network interface:** The data is copied from the kernel space to the network interface's buffers.

Similarly, when receiving data, the data is copied from the network interface to the kernel and then from the kernel to the application.

These data copying operations can add significant overhead, especially when dealing with large amounts of data. Zero-copy networking aims to eliminate these unnecessary copies, improving performance and reducing CPU utilization.

How Zero-Copy Networking Works

Zero-copy networking bypasses the copying of data to and from user space by allowing the operating system to transfer data directly from the kernel space to the network interface. This is typically achieved using specialized system calls and hardware support.

The key idea is to share memory between the application and the kernel, allowing the kernel to access the application's data directly without having to copy it. The kernel can then instruct the network interface to transmit the data from the shared memory region, eliminating the need for data copying.

Zero-Copy in Rust

Rust provides some support for zero-copy networking through system calls and libraries that expose zero-copy functionalities.

- sendfile(): This system call allows you to transfer data directly from a file to a socket, without copying the data to user space.

- mmap(): This system call allows you to map a file or a shared memory region into your application's address space, enabling direct access to the data.
- **Specialized libraries:** Some libraries, such as io_uring (Linux) and kqueue (macOS), provide mechanisms for performing zero-copy I/O operations.

Benefits of Zero-Copy Networking

Zero-copy networking offers several benefits:

- Improved performance: By eliminating data copying, zero-copy networking can significantly improve data transfer speed and reduce latency.
- Reduced CPU utilization: Zero-copy reduces the CPU overhead associated with data copying, freeing up CPU resources for other tasks.
- Increased throughput: Zero-copy can increase network throughput by allowing more data to be transferred in the same amount of time.

Real-World Examples

Zero-copy networking is used in various performance-critical applications:

- High-performance web servers: Web servers like Nginx use zero-copy to efficiently serve static files and handle high traffic loads.
- File transfer services: File transfer services like Dropbox use zero-copy to speed up file transfers and reduce server load.
- Streaming platforms: Streaming platforms like Netflix use zero-copy to efficiently deliver video content to users.
- Databases: Some databases use zero-copy to improve query performance and reduce disk I/O.

By understanding and utilizing zero-copy networking techniques in your Rust applications, you can achieve significant performance gains and build highly efficient network services. However, keep in mind that zero-copy might not be available or suitable for all situations, and it often requires careful consideration of system architecture and data management.

Chapter 11: Testing and Debugging

Testing and debugging are essential processes in software development that help us identify and fix these issues, ensuring that our applications are reliable, robust, and function as intended. Think of testing as a series of quality checks that we perform on our code. It's like inspecting a car before a long road trip to make sure everything is in good working order and prevent any breakdowns along the way. Debugging is like investigating a crime scene – we carefully examine the evidence (our code and its behavior) to identify the culprit (the bug) and bring it to justice (fix it).

In this chapter, we'll explore different testing techniques, including unit testing and integration testing, and learn about debugging tools and strategies that can help us track down and resolve issues in our Rust network applications.

11.1 Unit Testing

In network programming, unit tests are essential for verifying the correctness of our core networking logic, such as parsing network protocols, handling data serialization, and implementing algorithms for encryption or compression. By thoroughly testing these individual components, we can build a solid foundation for our network applications and prevent unexpected behavior or errors down the line.

How Unit Testing Works

Unit testing involves isolating and testing individual units of your code, such as functions or modules, in a controlled environment. The goal is to verify that each unit behaves as expected in various scenarios, including edge cases and invalid inputs.

A typical unit test consists of:

1. Setup: Preparing the necessary data and environment for the test.
2. Execution: Calling the function or method under test with specific inputs.
3. Assertion: Verifying that the output or behavior of the code matches the expected outcome.

Unit Testing in Rust

Rust provides excellent support for unit testing through the built-in test crate. This crate offers the #[test] attribute, which allows you to mark test functions. These test functions are automatically executed when you run a cargo test.

Here's a simple example:

Rust

```
#[cfg(test)]

mod tests {

    use super::*;

    #[test]

    fn test_parse_ip_address() {

        let ip_address = "192.168.1.1";

        let result = parse_ip_address(ip_address);

        assert!(result.is_ok());

        assert_eq!(result.unwrap(), "192.168.1.1");

    }
```

```
    #[test]
    fn test_parse_invalid_ip_address() {
        let ip_address = "invalid ip address";
        let result = parse_ip_address(ip_address);
        assert!(result.is_err());
    }
}

fn parse_ip_address(ip_address: &str) -> Result<String, String> {
    // ... implementation for parsing an IP address ...
}
```

In this example:

- We define a tests module to contain our test functions.
- The test_parse_ip_address function tests the parse_ip_address function with a valid IP address and asserts that the result is as expected.
- The test_parse_invalid_ip_address function tests the parse_ip_address function with an invalid IP address and asserts that the result is an error.

Benefits of Unit Testing

Unit testing offers numerous benefits for software development:

- Early bug detection: By testing individual units of code, you can identify and fix bugs early in the development process,

before they become more complex and challenging to track down.
- Improved code quality: Writing unit tests encourages you to write modular, well-defined, and testable code, leading to better code design and maintainability.
- Regression prevention: Unit tests act as a safety net, helping you prevent regressions (when code changes inadvertently break existing functionality) and ensure that your code remains stable and reliable over time.
- Documentation: Well-written unit tests can serve as documentation, demonstrating how your code is intended to be used and what its expected behavior is.
- Confidence in refactoring: Unit tests give you the confidence to refactor your code, knowing that if you break something, the tests will catch it.

Real-World Examples

Unit testing is a widely adopted practice in various software development domains:

- Networking libraries: Networking libraries, such as hyper and tokio, have extensive unit tests to ensure the correctness of their core functionalities.
- Cryptographic libraries: Cryptographic libraries, such as openssl and ring, rely heavily on unit tests to verify the correctness and security of their cryptographic algorithms.
- Embedded systems: Unit testing is crucial in embedded systems development to ensure the reliability and safety of embedded software, which often controls critical functionalities.

Incorporating unit testing into your Rust network programming workflow, you can build a solid foundation for your applications, ensure the correctness of your code, and create robust and reliable network services.

11.2 Integration Testing

While unit tests focus on verifying the correctness of isolated units of code, integration tests take a broader perspective and examine how different parts of our application work together as a cohesive whole.

Think of it like this: you've built a car by meticulously testing each component – the engine, the brakes, the transmission – in isolation. Now, it's time to take the car for a test drive to ensure that all those components work together harmoniously to propel the vehicle forward. Integration testing is that test drive for your software, ensuring that the different modules, components, or services interact correctly and produce the desired outcome.

Why Integration Testing Matters

In network programming, integration testing is particularly important because network applications often involve complex interactions between different parts of the system:

- Client-server communication: You need to ensure that the client and server can communicate correctly, exchange data seamlessly, and handle various network conditions.
- Microservices: If your application consists of multiple microservices, integration testing verifies that these services can interact correctly and exchange data as intended.
- External dependencies: Your application might interact with external services, such as databases or third-party APIs. Integration testing ensures that these interactions are handled correctly and that your application can gracefully handle different responses or errors from external services.

Writing Integration Tests in Rust

In Rust, you can write integration tests using the same test crate as unit tests. However, integration tests often require more setup and coordination to ensure that the different parts of the application are configured and interacting correctly.

Here's a basic example of an integration test for a client-server application:

Rust

```
#[cfg(test)]
mod tests {
    use super::*;
    use std::net::TcpStream;
    use std::io::{Read, Write};

    #[tokio::test]
    async fn test_client_server_communication() {
        // Start the server in a separate thread or task
        tokio::spawn(async {
            start_server().await;
        });

        // Wait for the server to start

        std::thread::sleep(std::time::Duration::from_millis(100));

        // Connect to the server
```

```rust
        let mut stream =
TcpStream::connect("127.0.0.1:8080").unwrap();

        // Send a message to the server

        stream.write_all(b"Hello").unwrap();

        // Receive the response from the server

        let mut buffer = [0; 5];

        stream.read_exact(&mut buffer).unwrap();

        // Assert that the response is as expected

        assert_eq!(&buffer, b"World");

    }

}

async fn start_server() {

    // ... server implementation ...

}
```

In this example:

- We start the server in a separate task using tokio::spawn().
- We wait for the server to start before connecting the client.
- The client connects to the server, sends a message, and receives a response.
- We assert that the response from the server matches the expected value.

Benefits of Integration Testing

Integration testing offers several benefits for building robust network applications:

- System-level validation: It ensures that the different parts of your application work together correctly and that the system as a whole functions as intended.
- End-to-end testing: It allows you to test the entire flow of your application, from user input to data processing to network communication, ensuring that all components are working together seamlessly.
- Realistic scenarios: Integration tests can be designed to simulate realistic user scenarios and test how your application handles different workloads, network conditions, and error situations.
- Increased confidence: Integration tests provide increased confidence in the reliability and stability of your application, as they verify that the system works correctly as a whole.

Real-World Examples

Integration testing is a crucial practice in various software development scenarios:

- Web applications: Integration tests are used to test the interaction between the frontend and backend of web applications, ensuring that data is exchanged correctly and that the user interface behaves as expected.
- Microservices: Integration tests are essential for verifying the communication and data exchange between different microservices in a distributed system.
- Embedded systems: Integration testing is used to test the interaction between embedded software and hardware components, ensuring that the system functions correctly in its intended environment.

Incorporating integration testing into your Rust network programming workflow, you can build robust and reliable applications that can handle complex interactions and provide a seamless user experience.

11.3 Debugging Techniques

Debugging is the detective work we do to track down these bugs, understand their root cause, and squash them once and for all. Think of debugging as solving a mystery. You're the detective, and the bug is the culprit. You need to gather clues, analyze the evidence, and use your deductive skills to identify the source of the problem and bring the perpetrator to justice (or, in our case, fix the bug).[3]

Debugging Tools and Techniques in Rust

Rust provides a variety of tools and techniques to help us in our debugging endeavors:[4]

- **println!** debugging: This is the classic debugging technique, and often the most effective. By strategically placing println! statements in your code, you can print out values of variables, trace the execution flow, and observe the state of your program at various points. It's like leaving breadcrumbs along the path of your program's execution to understand where things might be going wrong.
- Debugger: Rust supports debugging with tools like gdb (GNU Debugger) and lldb (LLDB debugger). These powerful debuggers allow you to step through your code line by line, inspect the values of variables, set breakpoints to pause execution at specific points, and analyze the program's state in detail. It's like having a magnifying glass and a time machine to examine your code's behavior under a microscope.

- Logging: Logging frameworks, such as the log crate and the more advanced tracing crate, allow you to record events and messages from your application. This can provide valuable insights into the behavior of your code, especially in complex or long-running applications. It's like having a detailed logbook of your application's activities, which can help you track down the sequence of events that led to an error.

Effective Debugging Strategies

Debugging is often an iterative process that involves a combination of techniques and strategies.[5] Here are some tips to help you become a master bug detective:

- Reproduce the bug consistently: The first step in debugging is to reliably reproduce the bug. This helps you understand the conditions under which the bug occurs and narrow down the potential causes. It's like recreating the crime scene to understand how the culprit committed the crime.
- Isolate the problem: Try to isolate the problematic code section or component by systematically eliminating potential causes and narrowing down the scope of your investigation.[6] It's like eliminating suspects one by one until you identify the true culprit.
- Use the scientific method: Formulate hypotheses about the cause of the bug, test those hypotheses by examining code, data, and logs, and refine your understanding based on the results.[7] It's like conducting experiments to gather evidence and support your conclusions.
- Read error messages carefully: Error messages often provide valuable clues about the cause of the problem.[8] Pay close attention to the error message, the line number where it occurred, and any relevant context provided. It's like reading the ransom note left by the culprit – it might contain subtle hints or clues.

- Ask for help: Don't be afraid to ask for help from colleagues, online communities, or documentation. A fresh perspective or a different approach can often help you spot the bug that you've been overlooking. It's like calling in reinforcements when you're stuck on a case.

Debugging Network Applications

Debugging network applications often presents unique challenges due to the distributed nature of the system.[9] Here are some additional tips for debugging network-related issues:

- Check network connectivity: Ensure that the network connection between the client and server is stable and that there are no network issues preventing communication.[10] It's like making sure the phone lines are working before trying to make a call.
- Inspect network traffic: Use tools like tcpdump or Wireshark to capture and analyze network traffic between the client and server. This can help you identify any unexpected messages, delays, or errors in the communication. It's like tapping the phone line to listen in on the conversation and identify any suspicious activity.
- Test with different network conditions: Simulate different network conditions, such as latency or packet loss, to see how your application behaves under stress.[11] It's like testing the car on different terrains to ensure it can handle various road conditions.
- Use logging strategically: Add logging statements to your code to track the flow of data and identify potential issues in the communication between the client and server. It's like leaving a trail of breadcrumbs to follow the path of the data as it travels through the network.

Mastering debugging techniques and utilizing the available tools, you can effectively track down and resolve bugs in your Rust network applications. This will help you build robust, reliable, and high-quality applications that can handle the complexities of the networked world.

Chapter 12: Deployment and Monitoring

Deploying an application involves making it available to users, whether it's on a web server, a cloud platform, or a distributed network. Think of it like launching a rocket into space. You've carefully designed and built the rocket, tested all its systems, and now it's time for the grand finale – the launch! Deployment is that launch for your application, sending it out into the world to fulfill its mission.

In this chapter, we'll explore how to deploy our Rust network applications to a server and discuss important aspects of monitoring and logging to ensure our applications run smoothly and efficiently in their new environment.

12.1 Deploying to a Server

Deploying an application involves making it accessible to users, whether it's on a web server, in the cloud, or across a distributed network. Think of it as the grand opening of your new restaurant – you've designed the menu, hired the staff, and set up the dining area, and now you're ready to open the doors and welcome your first customers.

Deploying a Rust network application can seem daunting, but with careful planning and the right tools, it can be a smooth and efficient process. Let's break down the key steps involved.

Choosing a Server Environment

First things first, you need to decide where your application will reside. This involves choosing a server environment that meets your application's specific needs and resource requirements. Here are some common options:

- Physical Server: This gives you maximum control over the hardware and software. You're responsible for maintaining the server, ensuring its security, and handling any issues that arise. This is often more expensive and requires technical expertise.
- Virtual Private Server (VPS): A VPS offers a good balance of control and affordability. It's a virtualized server that runs on a physical server, giving you dedicated resources and the ability to customize the environment. Popular VPS providers include DigitalOcean, Linode, and Vultr.
- Cloud Platform: Cloud platforms like Amazon Web Services (AWS), Microsoft Azure, and Google Cloud Platform (GCP) provide a wide range of services and infrastructure for deploying and managing applications. They offer scalability, flexibility, and pay-as-you-go pricing models.

The choice of server environment depends on several factors:

- Budget: Physical servers are generally the most expensive, followed by VPS, and then cloud platforms.
- Technical expertise: Managing a physical server requires more technical expertise than using a VPS or a cloud platform.
- Scalability: Cloud platforms offer the best scalability, allowing you to easily adjust resources as your application's needs change.
- Security: All options can be secure, but cloud platforms often have robust security measures in place.

Building and Packaging Your Application

Once you've chosen your server environment, it's time to prepare your application for deployment. This involves:

- Building for the Target Environment: You need to compile your Rust code for the target operating system and

architecture of your server. Cargo, Rust's build tool, supports cross-compilation, allowing you to build your application on your local machine for a different target platform.
- Packaging for Deployment: You might want to package your application into a distributable format, such as:
  - Standalone executable: You can create a single executable file that contains your application and all its dependencies. This makes it easy to deploy and run your application on the server.
  - Docker container: Docker containers provide a portable and isolated environment for your application. This ensures consistency across different server environments and simplifies dependency management.

Transferring and Installing

With your application built and packaged, you need to transfer it to your server. Common methods include:

- **scp** (secure copy): This command-line tool allows you to securely copy files over SSH.
- **rsync**: This tool efficiently synchronizes files between your local machine and the server, transferring only the changes.
- File transfer services: Services like FileZilla or SFTP clients provide graphical interfaces for transferring files.

Once your application is on the server, you need to:

- Install dependencies: If your application has external dependencies, you need to install them on the server. This might involve using a package manager like apt (on Debian/Ubuntu) or yum (on CentOS/RHEL).
- Configure the environment: You might need to configure environment variables, create directories, or set up permissions to ensure your application runs correctly.

Starting and Running

Finally, you need to start your application on the server. This might involve:

- Running as a service: You can configure your application to run as a background service that starts automatically when the server boots.
- Using a process manager: Process managers like systemd (on Linux) can help you manage and monitor your application.
- Running in a Docker container: If you've packaged your application in a Docker container, you can use Docker commands to start and manage the container.

Real-World Examples

Deployment practices vary depending on the application and the environment. Here are some examples:

- Web applications: Web applications are often deployed to web servers like Nginx or Apache, which handle incoming requests and forward them to your application.
- Microservices: Microservices are typically deployed in containers and orchestrated using tools like Kubernetes.
- Embedded systems: Embedded applications are deployed directly to the target device, such as a microcontroller or an embedded Linux system.

By carefully considering these steps and utilizing the appropriate tools and techniques, you can successfully deploy your Rust network applications to a server and make them available to your users.

12.2 Monitoring and Logging

Monitoring and logging are essential practices for maintaining the health, stability, and performance of our deployed applications.[1] They help us identify potential issues, diagnose problems, and ensure our applications are running smoothly.[2]

Monitoring

Monitoring involves collecting and analyzing data about your application's performance and behavior.[3] It's like having a dashboard that displays vital signs, such as CPU usage, memory consumption, network traffic, and request latency. This real-time information allows you to:

- Identify bottlenecks: Spot performance issues and identify areas where your application is struggling to keep up with demand.[4]
- Detect anomalies: Notice unusual patterns or spikes in activity that might indicate errors or potential problems.[5]
- Ensure optimal performance: Track key metrics and ensure your application is running efficiently and meeting performance expectations.[6]
- Make informed decisions: Use data to make informed decisions about scaling your application, optimizing resources, or troubleshooting issues.[7]

Monitoring Tools and Techniques

There are various tools and techniques available for monitoring your Rust network applications:

- System monitoring tools: Most operating systems provide built-in tools for monitoring system performance, such as CPU usage, memory usage, and network traffic. On Linux, tools like top, htop, and iostat can provide valuable insights into your server's resource utilization.

- Application performance monitoring (APM) tools: APM tools provide more comprehensive monitoring and insights into your application's performance.[8] They can track metrics like request latency, error rates, and database performance.[9] Popular APM tools include Datadog, New Relic, and Dynatrace.
- Prometheus: Prometheus is an open-source monitoring system and time series database.[10] It allows you to collect metrics from your application and define alerts based on those metrics. You can integrate Prometheus with Grafana to create dashboards and visualize your data.[11]
- Custom metrics: You can instrument your Rust application to collect custom metrics that are specific to your application's logic and functionality.[12] This can provide valuable insights into the inner workings of your application and help you identify areas for optimization.[13]

Logging: Recording Events and Insights

Logging involves recording events and messages from your application.[14] It's like keeping a detailed logbook of your application's activities, including information about requests, errors, warnings, and other noteworthy events. This logbook can be invaluable for:

- Understanding application behavior: Logs provide a historical record of your application's activity, allowing you to understand how it behaves under different conditions and identify patterns or trends.[15]
- Troubleshooting issues: When errors or unexpected behavior occur, logs can help you trace the sequence of events leading up to the problem, identify the root cause, and debug the issue.[16]
- Auditing and security analysis: Logs can be used for security auditing, intrusion detection, and compliance purposes.[17]

Logging in Rust

Rust provides excellent support for logging through crates like log and tracing:

- **log**: This crate provides a simple and widely used logging facade.[18] It allows you to log messages at different levels (error, warn, info, debug, trace) and send them to different log targets, such as the console or a file.
- **tracing**: This crate provides a more advanced and structured logging framework.[19] It allows you to capture structured data, create spans to trace the flow of execution, and integrate with various backends for log analysis and visualization.

Here's a simple example using the log crate:

Rust

```rust
use log::{info, error};

fn main() {
    env_logger::init(); // Initialize the logger

    info!("Starting the application...");

    // ... application logic ...

    if let Err(e) = some_function() {
        error!("An error occurred: {}", e);
    }
}
```

In this example, we initialize the env_logger (a simple logger that prints to the console) and log messages at the "info" and "error" levels.

Best Practices for Monitoring and Logging

- Choose the right tools: Select monitoring and logging tools that meet your application's needs and integrate well with your server environment.
- Establish clear log levels: Use different log levels to categorize messages based on their severity and importance.[20]
- Structure your logs: Use structured logging to capture relevant data and make it easier to analyze and query logs.[21]
- Centralize log storage: Store logs in a centralized location, such as a file, a database, or a log management service, for easier access and analysis.[22]
- Monitor key metrics: Identify the most critical metrics for your application and monitor them closely.[23]
- Set up alerts: Configure alerts to notify you of critical events or performance issues.

By effectively monitoring and logging your Rust network applications, you can gain valuable insights into their behavior, detect and resolve issues proactively, and ensure their smooth and efficient operation.

Conclusion

Congratulations! You've reached the end of this journey through the exciting world of Rust network programming. We've covered a lot of ground, from the fundamentals of networking to advanced concurrency patterns, security best practices, and performance optimization techniques. You've learned how to build robust and efficient network applications using Rust's powerful features and its rich ecosystem of libraries.

But this is just the beginning. The world of network programming is vast and ever-evolving. New technologies, protocols, and challenges emerge constantly, requiring us to adapt, learn, and refine our skills. The knowledge and skills you've gained from this book provide a solid foundation for further exploration and growth in this dynamic field.

As you continue your journey, remember the key principles we've emphasized throughout this book:

- Safety: Rust's focus on memory safety and concurrency safety empowers you to build reliable and secure network applications that are free from common pitfalls and vulnerabilities.
- Performance: Rust's zero-cost abstractions and efficient memory management allow you to create high-performance network applications that can handle demanding workloads and scale to meet the needs of modern networks.
- Concurrency: Rust's powerful concurrency features, including threads, asynchronous programming, and channels, enable you to build concurrent applications that can efficiently handle multiple connections and tasks.
- Security: By understanding and applying security best practices, such as TLS, encryption, authentication, and

authorization, you can protect your network applications and user data from various threats.
- Community: The Rust community is a vibrant and supportive group of developers who are passionate about building robust and reliable software. Engage with the community, share your knowledge, and learn from others to continue growing your skills.

The future of network programming is bright, and Rust is poised to play a significant role in shaping that future. With its unique combination of safety, performance, and expressiveness, Rust empowers you to build the next generation of network applications that are secure, efficient, and scalable.

So, go forth and build amazing things! The network awaits your creations.

www.ingramcontent.com/pod-product-compliance
Lightning Source LLC
Chambersburg PA
CBHW082245220526
45469CB00009B/2883